Streetwise

1 A Profile of Police Patrol

2 Police Patrol and Public Expectations

3 Managing Rising Demand

4 Direction and Targeting of Patrol

5 Police Patrol – the Way Forward

Contents

Preface	3
Summary	5
1 A Profile of Police Patrol	8
The office of constable	9
The organisation of patrol work	10
The purpose of patrol	12
2 Police Patrol and Public Expectations	16
Unrealistic expectations	17
Public preference for more foot patrol	19
Nuisance and anti-social behaviour – whose problem is it anyway?	20
3 Managing Rising Demand	22
Applying graded response	24
– Grading of emergency calls	24
– Police attendance at non-urgent incidents	25
– Supervision and monitoring in the control room	27
Matching resources to demand	29
– The use of supplementary provision	30
4 Direction and Targeting of Patrol	34
Objectives for patrol	35
– The difficulty of measuring patrol outcomes	36
Symptoms rather than causes – the short-term focus of patrol work	37
– Information and analysis needed for problem-solving	37
– Local identification and ownership	38
Briefing and debriefing of patrol officers	40
The status of beat work	41
Supervising patrol	42
– Tutoring of probationers	44

5 Police Patrol – the Way Forward	45
Action by the Home Office and police authorities	46
Community safety – putting patrol in context	48
Action by police forces – spreading good practice	50
– Managing demand – making graded response work	51
– Help desks	52
Matching resources to demand	55
– Shift patterns and abstractions	55
– Getting the best from additional contributions to patrol effort	55
– Candid cameras: the role of CCTV	59
– Auxiliary patrol officers	60
Targeting patrol work	61
– Setting clear objectives	61
– Using performance indicators to target patrol work and monitor achievement	62
– Encouraging a problem-solving approach	64
– Geographic policing	64
– Improving briefings and tasking	66
Raising the status of patrol and enhancing supervision	67
– Leadership on the streets: supervision and tutoring	68

Recommendations	70
To the Home Office and police authorities	70
To the public	70
To police forces	71
Appendix 1	
Forces visited during the study	73
Appendix 2	
Members of Advisory Panel and Working Group	74
Appendix 3	
Surveys and questionnaires	75
Appendix 4	
'Bounty' payments to Special Constables	77
References	79
Index	80

© Crown Copyright 1996

Applications for reproduction should be made to HMSO

Printed in the UK for the Audit Commission by Colourcraft, Cardiff

ISBN 011 866 418 1

London HMSO

Photographs by kind permission of:
Hilary Shedel (cover, p8, p22, p31, p33, p34, p52, p55, p59, p69); Hulton Deutsch (p3); Image Bank (p5); Photofusion (p7); Format (pp14-15); Northumbria Police (p16); Metropolitan Police (p45)

Preface

The uniformed constable on patrol has long been the traditional symbol of British policing, held in high regard by the public. But patrol work has changed radically in recent decades. This report examines how well police forces are coping with the challenges posed by a rising level of demand as policing becomes ever broader in scope. It focuses on the management of police activities and resources, but relates this to public expectations and the role of other agencies in helping to maintain safe communities.

The report is based on a study that involved in-depth fieldwork in five provincial police forces in England and Wales, covering all aspects of patrol, with shorter visits to ten other forces to look at specific issues such as partnership initiatives, beat managers and the use of information technology. The forces visited are named in Appendix 1; the Commission would like to express its gratitude for their co-operation. In addition, the National Audit Office (NAO) carried out elements of the fieldwork in the Metropolitan Police Service (MPS). This is the first major police study on which the Audit Commission and the NAO have collaborated in this way, and both the NAO's contribution and the co-operation of the MPS are gratefully acknowledged.

The fieldwork was supplemented by data analysis, a public survey conducted on the Commission's behalf by MORI, a questionnaire completed by almost 500 patrol constables and sergeants in the six fieldwork forces, and a questionnaire completed by over 100 basic command units, spread across every provincial force in England and Wales. Examples of good practice by named forces are cited in this report; this is for the purposes of illustration and does not imply that only those forces have implemented these procedures.

The study team benefited considerably from professional guidance offered by an Advisory Panel of four chief constables and a Working Group (Appendix 2), together with advice from individual officers too numerous to mention. Particular assistance was provided by the Patrol Working Group of the Association of Chief Police Officers (ACPO), Her Majesty's Inspectorate of Constabulary (HMIC), the Police Superintendents' Association and the Police Federation. The Commission is grateful to these organisations, and all the other groups and individuals who commented on drafts of this report. As always, responsibility for the conclusions and recommendations rests with the Commission alone.

The study team comprised Kate Flannery from the Local Government Studies Directorate and Steve Jackson, seconded from District Audit, under the direction of Steve Evans. Inspector Huw Evans, on secondment from Hertfordshire Constabulary, provided valuable professional insights to the fieldwork and analysis stages, and additional research and interviewing were carried out by Lucy McCulloch, Clare Weiss, Angie Smith and Steve Sullivan.

This report concentrates on the study findings from a national perspective. It will be complemented by:

◆ an *Executive Briefing*, summarising the key findings and recommendations for senior police officers, police authority members and policy makers;

◆ a *Management Handbook*, which will set out an agenda for change within individual forces based on the detailed findings of the study research, and identify opportunities for local improvement; and

◆ an *Audit Guide*, to help police authorities' external auditors work with individual police forces in reviewing their performance locally and identifying where good practices in other forces can be adopted. Auditors will be carrying out this work in most forces during 1996 and preparing reports for police authorities.

Summary

'...there is a mismatch between what the public wants and what the police can deliver.'

The police, like other parts of the public sector, face competing demands for their services. They are expected to tackle crime effectively and provide a fast response to emergencies, while at the same time meeting an almost insatiable public appetite for visible patrol – 'bobbies on the beat'. Taking a broad definition of patrol, including response to incidents and specialisms such as traffic patrol, this area of policing absorbs around 60 per cent of resources, at an annual cost of £4 billion. Patrol officers are the front line and public face of policing. As rising demand puts pressure on police managers, it is appropriate to ask whether forces – and the public – are getting the best from this expenditure.

Surveys consistently show that the public attaches great value to police patrol. It provides a sense of security and symbolises lawful authority at a time when there are increasing concerns about an erosion of authority. So it is a matter of concern that, despite a high degree of satisfaction with most aspects of policing, the Commission's own survey of the public's views reinforces the message of dissatisfaction with current levels of foot patrol. Why, despite their best intentions, are the police not meeting public expectations in this key area?

This study has highlighted three key points:

◆ public expectations are not wholly realistic;

◆ in many forces there are opportunities to manage existing demand better; officers spend much of their available time awaiting deployment to incidents or dealing with incidents which do not merit police attendance; and

◆ what time there is between incidents is not always used effectively, and could be better targeted and more productive.

Police resources are spread thinly given the territory they cover. Even if they did nothing other than patrol the streets, forces could not provide the level of cover that the public would ideally like. And putting all available officers out on patrol would undermine strategies to tackle crime, which require a high degree of specialisation in non-uniformed work. So there is a mismatch between what the public wants and what the police can deliver.

The need to provide 24-hour cover and meet various specialist demands means that, at any one time, only around 5 per cent of a force's total strength is actually patrolling the streets. It is essential, therefore, that these officers work efficiently and productively, especially given the expectations held of them by the public.

Currently, however, patrol effort in many forces can be characterised as 'fire-brigade policing'. It is highly reactive and patrol officers spend a significant proportion of their time – up to 60 per cent in some areas – dealing with incidents and their aftermath. One explanation is the steep rise in the

5

'...foot patrol is not a panacea for all policing problems...'

number of incidents; another is inadequate decision-making in the control room, the heart of police operations. For example, some forces are not grading incidents according to the urgency of the required response in the way intended by force policy. Many incidents are graded as emergencies when they are not, and officers are sent to some where attendance is not likely to be fruitful. Forces are also missing opportunities to make the best use of supplementary effort, notably that of Special Constables. In addition, non-incident time is not used as productively as it could be. This is because clear objectives are not usually set for patrol officers, briefings are variable in quality and debriefings rare, and because most forces have poor systems to collect and analyse information.

To secure improvement in performance and increase public satisfaction, action is required by government, police authorities and the public, to:

◆ be more realistic about what the police should be expected to provide; a public information campaign about what type of calls it is appropriate for the police to handle, and when to use the 999 system, could help. Also, the public and politicians need to understand that foot patrol is *not* a panacea for all policing problems;

◆ consider the costs and benefits of a multi-agency helpline, offering advice and information across the spectrum of local authority, health, utilities and police services – perhaps using a 333 number or equivalent – to ease the burden of non-urgent calls on police control rooms;

◆ encourage better communication between police and local communities, to reach a shared perception of problems that merit police attention;

◆ consider putting partnership work by local authorities and other public sector bodies on a statutory footing, to improve the co-ordination between different agencies on community safety issues; and

◆ consider paying Special Constables, and revise national conditions regulating the shift systems of police to give greater flexibility.

A number of recommended actions fall within the remit of forces themselves, specifically to:

◆ help shape public expectations so that they are closer to what forces can deliver;

◆ get closer to communities – understand better what problems disturb them and respond appropriately; ensure that at least some patrol effort accords with the principles of 'geographic policing', in which officers are assigned to particular localities;

◆ 'work smarter rather than harder' – grade incidents properly, try to resolve more problems at the first attempt and reduce the number of repeat visits by patrol officers;

◆ encourage patrol supervisors to spend more time out on the streets;

◆ exploit supplementary provision to the full, in the form of closed-circuit television (CCTV), Special Constables and multi-agency partnerships;

◆ set specific objectives and targets so that officers are clear what patrol is meant to achieve, and monitor progress in achievement.

It is a tribute to the commitment and professionalism of patrol officers that their role continues to be valued so highly by the public. Visible patrol, on foot and in cars, is integral to the style of policing in this country – at its best, it delivers key operational objectives and fosters good community relations. But variations in performance across the country show that there is room for improvement. If all forces adopt the good practices identified in this report, the traditions of the 'bobby on the beat' and policing by consent can be sustained and public reassurance strengthened.

1 A Profile of Police Patrol

The number of police officers has increased steadily this century to a figure of one officer for every 400 citizens.

Changes in urbanisation, mobility and telecommunications, combined with a marked rise in reported crime, have changed the nature of policing significantly.

Patrol costs about £4 billion a year. The nature of policing means that, at any one time, only around 5 per cent of police strength is actually patrolling the streets.

Members of the public attach great importance to foot patrol because it reassures them – but they also expect the police to deal with crime and respond quickly to emergencies.

The office of constable

1. The office of constable dates back 700 years, when the Statute of Winchester (1285) provided for two constables to be appointed by each Hundred to maintain law and order as agents of the local sheriff. Not until 1735 were London parishes allowed to pay their 'watch constables' from local taxes, and the modern constabulary dates from 1829, when London constables began to be paid and properly trained, although it took many decades before these changes were made across the country. The number of police officers has grown steadily throughout this century, from 45,000 in 1900 to the current figure of 127,000, although officers now work fewer hours, in common with other members of the working population. Over this time the ratio of police officers to population has improved gradually to 2.45 officers per 1,000 population (Exhibit 1), or roughly one officer for every 400 citizens.

2. For the first half of the century foot patrol was the constable's dominant activity, together with some crime work. Rural constables lived in the areas they patrolled and, until the early 1970s, were on 24-hour call; urban constables walked beats organised around fixed locations, or points, where they would meet their sergeant or call the station for instructions. Post-war shifts of population from crowded inner-city areas to suburbs and new towns, an increase in car ownership and thus mobility, greater use of telephones, and a marked rise in reported crime and other calls on the police have been important factors forcing changes in traditional styles of policing, especially in urban areas.

3. The changing world was reflected in changes to police organisation and patrolling methods. In particular, the introduction in the 1960s of personal radios, and an increasing use of cars to patrol areas much larger than the

Exhibit 1
Police strength since 1900

The number of police officers per 1,000 population has risen from 1.46 in 1900 to 2.45 in 1995; the low point in recent decades was the early 1950s, nostalgically viewed by some as a 'golden era'.

Police officers per 1,000 population

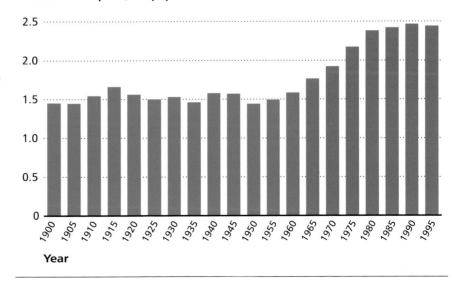

Year

Sources: Home Office and HMIC statistics for England and Wales

traditional beat, transformed the nature of patrol work. Officers became less familiar with their 'patches' and spent more of their duty time driving from one incident to another. The resulting loss of personal contact with the public and the decline of a visible police presence walking the streets weakened the relationship between the police and the communities they served. Since the early 1980s, forces have been making concerted efforts to re-establish these community links.

The organisation of patrol work

4. The police have difficult judgements to make about the priorities they give to the numerous demands made on them – principally to prevent and detect crime, patrol the streets and react to emergencies. Policing is now a highly specialised service, although uniformed patrol officers remain the principal resource and are the front-line, public face of the police. Typically, around 55 per cent of force strength is classed by HMIC as operational patrol, with a further 7 per cent in specialist traffic patrol (Exhibit 2). Thus, at current figures, patrol and support for it accounts for around 60 per cent of police resources, costing £4 billion in England and Wales in 1995/96.

5. However, the number of officers that a force is able to deploy on the streets at any one time is considerably less than 60 per cent of strength, for three main reasons. Firstly, the broad category of operational patrol includes specialised roles such as custody sergeant or child protection officer which are vital support to the patrol function but not seen by most members of the public. Secondly, policing is a round-the-clock service and patrol strength is divided into four shifts to cover (typically) three eight-hour blocks of duty plus rest days. Thirdly, front-line officers are away from rostered duties for planned reasons such as training and leave, and unplanned reasons such as sickness or late calls for court attendance.

6. These factors mean that a force can expect to have 10 per cent of its total strength available for routine patrol at any given time, supplemented by specialists such as mounted officers and public order teams. Even this number overstates the visible presence on the streets, because some on-duty time is necessarily spent in the police station – interviewing prisoners, completing paperwork, taking a meal break and so on. In practice, therefore, the nature of the service dictates that typically around 5 per cent of police strength is actually out on patrol at any one time. For an average-sized force of 2,500, this means 125 officers to serve a local population of around one million people (Exhibit 3). Most of those officers will be in cars, and will have to respond to incidents and other calls.

Exhibit 2
Police resources

Patrol accounts for just over 60 per cent of total police strength, including traffic officers.

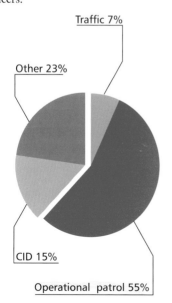

Traffic 7%

Other 23%

CID 15%

Operational patrol 55%

Source: Audit Commission analysis of Home Office and HMIC data, 1994

Exhibit 3
Officer deployment in a typical force

The nature of policing means that, at any one time, around 5 per cent of total strength is actually patrolling the streets.

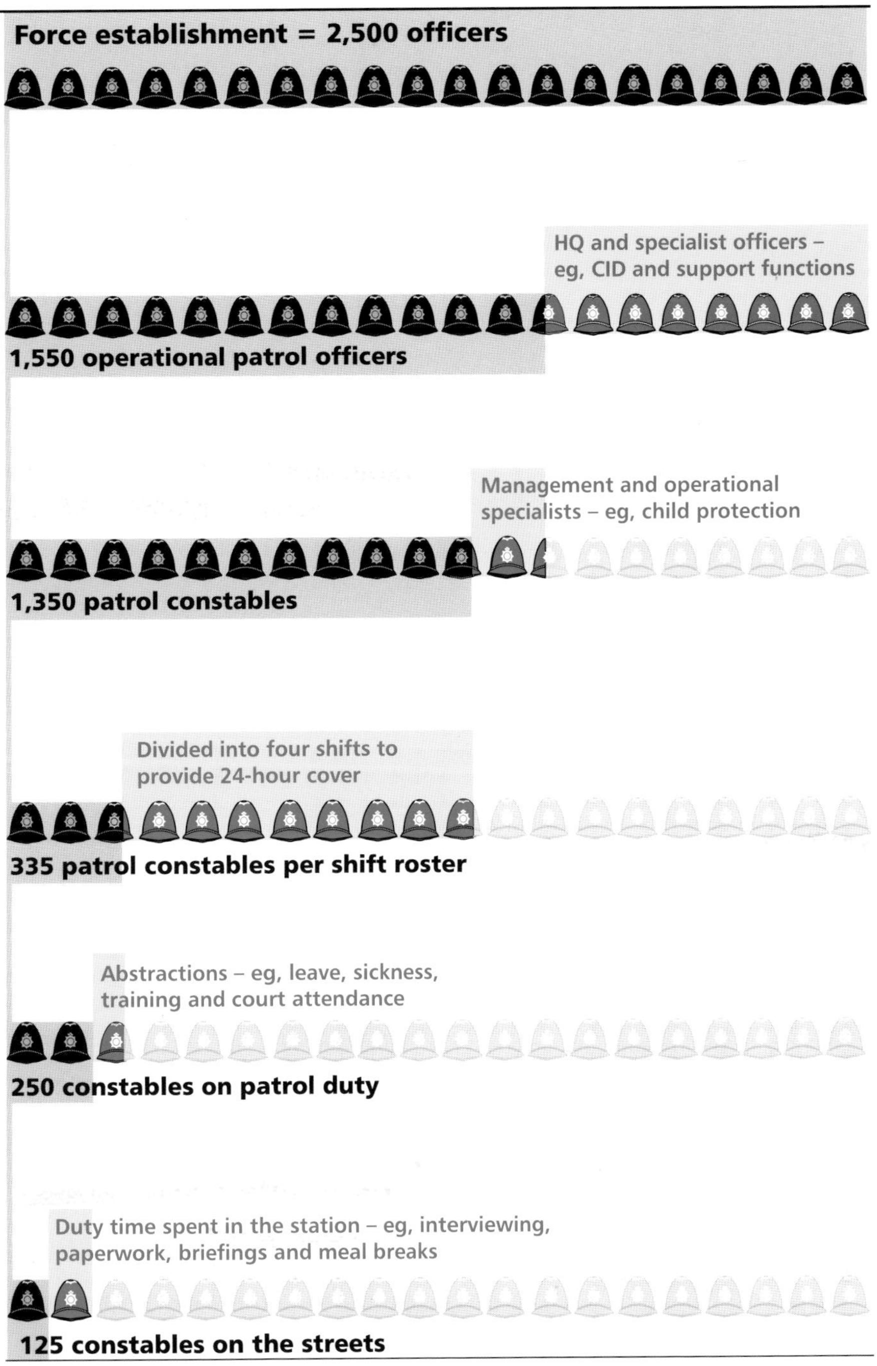

Force establishment = 2,500 officers

HQ and specialist officers – eg, CID and support functions

1,550 operational patrol officers

Management and operational specialists – eg, child protection

1,350 patrol constables

Divided into four shifts to provide 24-hour cover

335 patrol constables per shift roster

Abstractions – eg, leave, sickness, training and court attendance

250 constables on patrol duty

Duty time spent in the station – eg, interviewing, paperwork, briefings and meal breaks

125 constables on the streets

Source: Audit Commission analysis

The purpose of patrol

7. Police patrol is far more than a uniformed constable walking the streets. It is the principal, though not the only, means by which the police:

- respond appropriately to crimes, other incidents and emergencies;

- maintain public order and tackle anti-social behaviour;

- reassure the public through a visible police presence;

- forge links with local communities to reduce problems of crime and nuisance;

- gather intelligence, especially in relation to crime and criminals.

The first two types of patrol activity can loosely be described as reactive, in that they are driven primarily by incidents, while the other three are more proactive. Partly because of this range of key activities, there has until recently been no agreed definition of patrol nor, more importantly, consensus about what it is meant to achieve. In fact, there has long been debate as to whether patrol is a task in itself, or a tool to achieve specific objectives.

8. The other reason why a definition is hard to pin down is the complex and interrelated nature of patrol work – it cannot readily be split into discrete tasks and then assigned to different officers. For example, the single act of arresting someone committing a serious public nuisance could fulfil all five of these objectives at once. An officer on patrol may, while on an apparently routine patrol of the high street, be first on the scene of a fatal accident, or apprehend a street robber.

9. Much of this complexity is veiled from public view – for most people, the officer on foot patrol is still the resonant image. Survey after survey of the public repeats the demand for an increased visible police presence. In a recent nationwide poll conducted on behalf of the Police Federation,[I] 80 per cent of people said they wanted more police officers patrolling their area. Only one person in a hundred wanted less patrol. Patrols provide a sense of security, of help being close at hand, and they symbolise lawful authority. Foot patrol is especially important to people, largely due to a strongly held conviction that having police officers walk the streets not only makes them more accessible but also deters crime. 'More bobbies on the beat' has become a clarion call to which many police managers respond that they lack sufficient resources, given all the other demands upon them. Given this public appetite for a visible presence, it is a concern – though not a surprise – that a survey conducted for the Audit Commission[II] shows dissatisfaction with current levels of foot patrol (Exhibit 4 and Box A, overleaf).

I
Survey of Public Attitudes to Policing, Police Federation, May 1995; the survey was based on 1,000 street interviews.

II
The Audit Commission appointed MORI to interview in their homes a quota sample of 800 people, covering issues such as visibility of patrol officers, reassurance and satisfaction. See Appendix 3 for details of the sample size and methodology.

10. In analysing why, despite their best intentions, the police are unable to fulfil public expectations in the key area of foot patrol, three factors emerge:

◆ firstly, the expectations of the public are not wholly realistic, in that people want more than the police can actually deliver;

◆ secondly, in many forces the police are not managing the rising demand as well as they could. Officers spend much of their available time awaiting deployment to incidents or dealing with incidents that do not merit police attendance;

◆ thirdly, what time there is between incidents is not always used effectively; it could be better targeted and have more impact on the public.

11. Patrol is a cornerstone of effective policing – it either delivers or contributes significantly to every aspect of core police work, and is integral to the tradition of policing by consent on which a significant element of police effectiveness depends. In the past, the service has demonstrated the professionalism and commitment to rise to challenges such as those described above. This report is intended to assist the process by highlighting improvements that can be made to key aspects of patrol and encouraging the spread of existing good practice.

Exhibit 4
Public satisfaction with policing

People are highly satisfied with most police work – much of which is undertaken by patrol officers – but much less satisfied with levels of foot patrol.

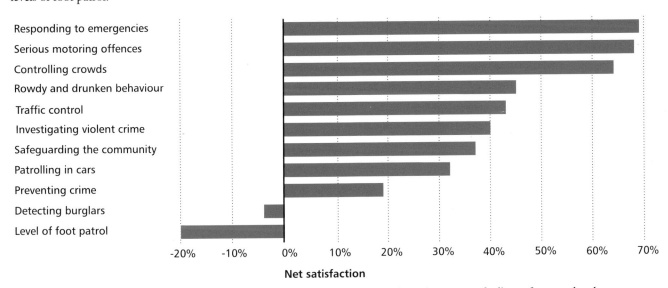

Note: The term 'net satisfaction' denotes the percentage expressing satisfaction with the various aspects of police performance less the percentage who say they are dissatisfied; a satisfaction level of 80% and a dissatisfaction level of 20% produce a net satisfaction figure of 60%.

Source: Survey of 800 people conducted by MORI on behalf of the Audit Commission

Box A
Public attitudes to police patrol

Views of police performance

• Overall, people were most positive about police response to emergencies

• They were less satisfied with levels of foot patrol and detecting burglaries

• Older residents and those in rural areas are most positive about overall performance

Paying for patrol

 • 3 in 5 say they would pay more tax to increase patrols

• 1 in 5 would pay for private patrols

• If some police work has to be reduced to increase patrols, traffic policing is the favoured area for cuts*

Priorities for improving community safety

• Better parental discipline and greater individual responsibility are the public's top priorities

• Well-lit streets and CCTV make people feel safer

• Those with children are most keen on CCTV

* The public may not fully understand traffic patrol's contribution to reducing crime and accidents and to providing a fast response to emergencies.

Source: MORI public survey conducted on behalf of the Audit Commission

Visibility and recognition

- 1 in 3 had seen officers on patrol in the past week
- In rural areas **22%** had spoken to a patrol officer, but only **3%** in inner cities
- 1 in 4 knows that an officer/team is responsible for patrol in that area

Nature of reassurance

- The sight of a patrol officer is always reassuring to 72% of people; a further 16% are reassured if they feel vulnerable **16% 72%**
- Patrol officers reassure because:
  - they represent law and order, so deter crime
  - they are close at hand in an emergency
- Seeing patrols makes drivers more careful

Key times and places

- Pubs and clubs at closing time were most often cited as needing patrol attention
- Almost half of parents rate patrols at schools as very important
- Large housing estates are a priority for **40%**
- Roads were cited as the least important location for patrol presence*

Public expectations about how many officers should be on foot patrol, and what they can achieve, are not wholly realistic. For example, officers on foot cannot generally provide a rapid response to incidents.

Crime accounts for only 30 per cent of calls for police service; police officers are increasingly being asked to deal with other problems such as nuisance and anti-social behaviour.

2 Police Patrol and Public Expectations

12. Police forces are increasingly responsive to public expectations, and have in recent years made great strides in improving procedures for consulting local communities. Local Policing Plans, prepared jointly with police authorities, are a potentially valuable means of establishing accountability for the services provided and the standards achieved. All Local Policing Plans must incorporate the Home Secretary's key objectives, one of which is 'to provide high visibility policing so as to reassure the public'. Achievement will be monitored by surveying public satisfaction with levels of both foot and mobile patrol. So although it has always been on their agenda, forces are to be held to account more publicly for their performance in this area. But in striving to increase reassurance and satisfaction, forces confront three pressing problems:

- public expectations of visible patrol, especially on foot, are not wholly realistic, in respect of both the number of officers that can be assigned to patrol and also what these officers can actually achieve;

- public dissatisfaction relates not only to the level of patrol but also *how* the police do it – in particular, the balance struck between foot and mobile patrol; and

- many calls attended by patrol officers relate to nuisance and anti-social behaviour, which are difficult to resolve. The public and the police do not always share an understanding of what constitutes a problem for which police attention is appropriate, or of where the responsibility for identifying a permanent resolution lies.

Unrealistic expectations

13. Patrol resources are spread very thinly given the territory they cover. This can be illustrated by looking at the statistics for a typical police area, divided into a number of beats for patrolling purposes. Each beat contains thousands of houses and businesses, whose occupants all want to see an officer passing by, and hundreds of miles of pavements, but the whole area is covered by only a handful of officers on patrol at any one time (Exhibit 5, overleaf). Police omnipresence is clearly not possible. Patrol levels are therefore never likely to achieve satisfaction ratings approaching 100 per cent, unless the police moderate public expectations by explaining how thinly the 'blue line' is actually stretched. However, the police are often reluctant to do this lest they undermine the very thing they are striving to provide – public reassurance.

14. Is the answer to reduce the level of behind-the-scenes work and put more officers on street patrol duties? Forces are under pressure to do just this, but again the reality is more complex. The need for reassurance patrol coexists with other major demands, measured principally in terms of success in tackling crime and the time taken to respond to emergencies. Effective police action against crime requires specialisation of roles – detectives, intelligence officers, scientific support and so on. Returning all of these officers to uniformed patrol duties would wreak havoc on a crime strategy,[1] and quickly reduce public confidence in the police. The police do not handle response to emergencies in the same way as the fire and ambulance services do, by posting crews to stations or strategic locations to await the next call – they combine it with the other patrol functions set out earlier. Currently, about 80 per cent of urgent

[1]
The Commission's report, *Helping with Enquiries: Tackling Crime Effectively*, 1993, examined crime strategies; one of its key recommendations was that specialist functions such as intelligence and crime pattern analysis should be strengthened. That does not ignore the important role played by uniformed officers, who in many forces investigate 60-80 per cent of all crime.

Exhibit 5
Patrolling a typical town

At any one time, there are only a few officers patrolling the streets of a typical town.

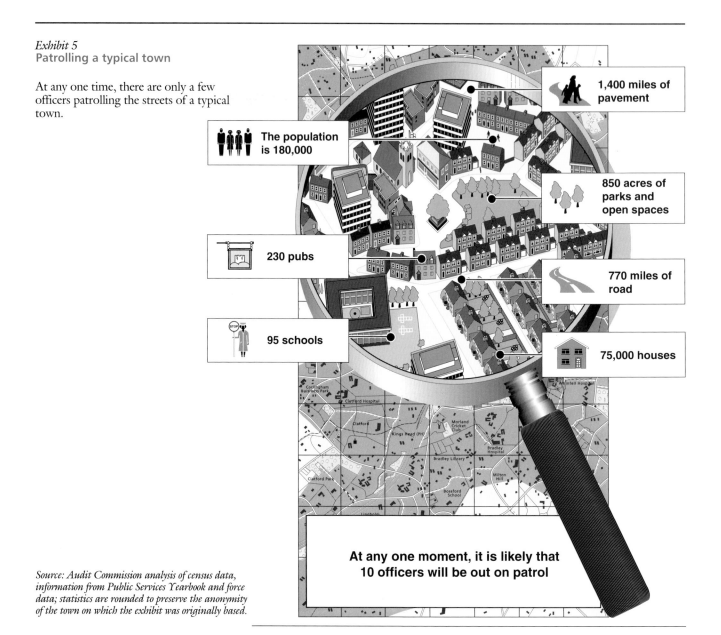

The population is 180,000

230 pubs

95 schools

1,400 miles of pavement

850 acres of parks and open spaces

770 miles of road

75,000 houses

At any one moment, it is likely that 10 officers will be out on patrol

Source: Audit Commission analysis of census data, information from Public Services Yearbook and force data; statistics are rounded to preserve the anonymity of the town on which the exhibit was originally based.

calls are attended within ten minutes. To improve response times substantially, forces might need to increase the number of officers crewing fast-response cars; this would reduce foot patrol levels even further and consequently erode the reassurance that foot patrol provides.

Public preference for more foot patrol

15. Forces that are able to increase the number of officers available for uniformed patrol by efficiency measures such as civilianisation, or reducing the paperwork burden, may find that increased public satisfaction does not automatically follow. One of the findings of the Commission's survey of the public is that patrol visibility in itself does not correlate with overall satisfaction with the police. People in the area where the highest proportion reported that they had seen officers on patrol within the previous few days were least positive about the overall performance of their local police. In part, this may be because there are more police in areas where crime and disorder impinge on daily life, notably in big cities, and thus the 'feel-good' factor is low.

16. But as well as this missing 'feel-good' factor, the lack of correlation may also derive from the balance that forces strike between deploying officers on foot and in cars. Among the fieldwork forces, on one day taken as a snapshot illustration, the percentage of patrol constables whose main type of duty was foot patrol varied from 23 per cent to less than 1 per cent. Although the public would rather see police officers in cars than not at all, the strong preference is for foot patrol. The Commission's survey explored this issue with a number of focus groups.[I] Group members emphasised two points. Firstly, mobile patrol symbolises high-speed, reactive policing. In the words of one member, 'They tend to be going to a crime rather than preventing one'. Secondly, officers in cars are less approachable and fail to get to know the local community well. Bobbies walking the beat, by contrast, 'have got time to stop and say "hello" and get to know you'. They are not perceived to be just a friendly face; unprompted, many participants also cited their effectiveness, 'They can feel the atmosphere, spot trouble at 20 paces, look down side streets ... they provide more complete coverage'.

17. However, police managers still have to grapple with the competing pressures of the public's demands for response and deterrence. Officers on foot could not get to the scene of an emergency within the common target time of ten minutes unless, by chance, they were patrolling within a few hundred metres of the incident. Many offences are committed stealthily, often in private places such as homes and shops, and much criminal behaviour is also opportunistic. Well-directed patrolling can reduce some criminal and anti-social behaviour, including vandalism, but there is little empirical evidence that marginal increases in patrol levels have a substantial impact upon the incidence of certain high-profile crimes such as burglary.[II] Furthermore, it is unrealistic to expect that crimes such as fraud or domestic violence could be much deterred or detected simply by police officers walking the area. Foot patrol clearly cannot be a cure-all for every policing problem, and it cannot be very effective as visible reassurance in sparsely populated areas.

I

Six focus groups were convened in three police force areas to discuss over a period of several hours a range of issues relating to reassurance and police patrol. The composition of the groups took account of differences in perspective that may arise from age, gender, ethnic origin and social class; see Appendix 3.

II

An exception is where police have deployed intensive or saturation levels of patrol eg, during a major enquiry, but this cannot be sustained for any length of time, and may simply displace crime. See David Bayley, *Police for the Future*, OUP, 1994, for a discussion of initiatives in patrolling.

Nuisance and anti-social behaviour – whose problem is it anyway?

18. Surveys of the public about the level and impact of patrol highlight an issue of growing difficulty for both police officers and local communities – dealing with nuisance and anti-social behaviour. Forces' surveys of crime victims reveal that even where the offence is not detected, the majority of victims are highly satisfied with the competence and courtesy shown by patrol officers. But crime, which everyone agrees is police business, accounts for only around 30 per cent of calls to police control rooms (Exhibit 6). A significant part of the police workload relates to a grey area of nuisance or anti-social behaviour – youths congregating on street corners, irresponsible parking, excessive noise and so on – not all of which is criminal. Changes in society, such as an erosion of respect for authority and a decline in neighbourliness, have reduced the capacity or willingness of communities to solve such problems without police intervention. Allying these changes to a major expansion of telecommunications, and thus access to the police, raises the concern that the service is becoming one of first, rather than last, resort.

19. Calls about nuisance comprise on average around 10 per cent of calls to police control rooms, though in some areas the proportion approaches 20 per cent. Dissatisfaction with the response by patrol officers may arise for two reasons. First, some officers may convey an impression that they resent having to deal with such 'trivia' when there are serious crimes to attend to – the matter does not reflect their view of what constitutes 'real policing'. This is a cultural issue which managers can address. The second, more intractable, cause of dissatisfaction can be that even when officers do respond sympathetically, they may be ineffectual because the solution to the problem lies not in law enforcement but in social measures such as new recreational facilities for youths, or in civil remedies.

20. Communities want action on these issues, as evidenced, for example, by the topics dominating local consultative groups set up under Section 106 of the Police and Criminal Evidence Act 1984 (Table 1). Although they may be called to the scene by members of the public, patrol officers are often unable to remedy the situation because the main responsibility for, and resources needed to resolve the problems lie elsewhere – with the local authority, the health authority or other agencies. This situation is as frustrating for the police as it is for the public.

Exhibit 6
Calls to control rooms

Calls to report crimes account for only 30 per cent of calls to police control rooms.

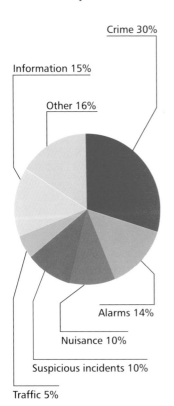

Crime 30%

Information 15%

Other 16%

Alarms 14%

Nuisance 10%

Suspicious incidents 10%

Traffic 5%

Source: Audit Commission analysis of fieldwork data in five provincial forces

Table 1
Issues most commonly raised by members of the public at Section 106 meetings

1	**Juvenile nuisance and anti-social behaviour***
2	**Burglary**
3	**Parking problems – eg, parking on grass verges**
4	**Environmental problems – eg, dogs fouling the pavement, noise**
5	**Vandalism and graffiti**
6	**Police presence – desire to see more officers on the beat**

* The public clearly does not think that juvenile nuisance is more serious than, say, murder or rape, but people are most likely to express concern about the kind of incidents which they witness most frequently or which they feel are not dealt with satisfactorily.

Source: Audit Commission analysis of agendas and minutes from provincial fieldwork sites over a period of six to nine months, 1994/95

21. The problems for forces posed by the weight of what, at times, are unrealistic expectations are considerable, and police efforts to address them are commendable. But some forces could follow the example of the best forces by improving performance in managing the response to rising demand – incident workload – and ensuring that non-incident time is targeted towards the achievement of key objectives.

3 Managing Rising Demand

Many forces are locked into a pattern of reactive, 'fire-brigade' policing in which responding to incidents squeezes out foot patrol, work with local communities and proactive patrolling.

This trend is only partly explained by rising demand. There are significant variations between forces in the application of graded response, which affects the way that patrol officers are deployed. Good practice in control rooms is not universal.

Demand varies by time of day, but shift systems do not always ensure that the right number of officers are on duty when they are most needed. Sickness absence is a significant drain on patrol strength. Some forces are missing opportunities to make the best use of Special Constables.

22. The police are a 24-hour, mobile emergency service, available to deal with almost any problem presented to them by a member of the public. Indeed, calls from the public are the principal demand on patrol officers, and the reactive nature of much patrol work is thus both inevitable and appropriate. But this reactivity can become a problem if patrol officers' time is dominated by attending, or awaiting deployment to, one incident after another. In this highly reactive style of policing, contact with local communities, proactivity and reassurance patrol will be squeezed out. One factor cited to explain this 'fire-brigade' pattern of policing is the rising demand for police services (Exhibit 7). Towns and cities have become choked by heavier traffic, crime levels almost doubled in the 14 years to 1994, while 999 calls have risen by around 150 per cent. These changes far outstrip the 8 per cent increase in the number of police officers over the period and have helped create what is seen as a growing demand gap.

23. However, rising demand alone cannot adequately explain why many patrol officers are trapped in a highly reactive pattern of work. Firstly, some forces have been more successful than others in avoiding fire-brigade policing – they have absorbed the rise in demand without sacrificing community-based, proactive patrol. Secondly, conventional workload measures – principally crimes and other calls for service per officer – do not bear out patrol officers' complaints that they are over-burdened by incidents. These statistics need careful interpretation as they give only part of the picture; not all work is generated by logged incidents, for example, and average figures mask the peaks of workload that can create problems. Nevertheless, analysis of data from a control room in a town centre revealed a workload per patrol officer per shift of 1.7 incidents, which included 0.25 arrests (ie, one arrest every four shifts), and 0.4 crime reports submitted. These statistics are consistent with national averages of, for example, around 1.4 incidents per patrol officer per shift.

Exhibit 7
The increase in workload per police officer, 1980 to 1994

Police strength has risen, but demand has grown at a much faster rate and workload per officer has increased.

Sources: Department of Transport, Home Office statistics, Audit Commission research

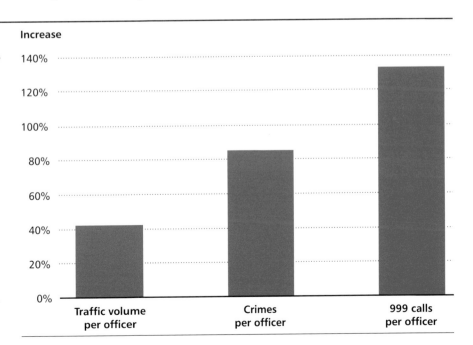

24. Interviews with patrol officers show that some of them are undoubtedly experiencing pressure. But forces need to consider whether this is in part generated by the way that they are managing demand. Findings from fieldwork and analysis suggest that there are significant variations in:

◆ applying graded response, which affects the way that patrol officers are deployed;

◆ matching resources to demand, through appropriate shift patterns and the use of Special Constables.

If forces can, where necessary, improve performance in these areas they will increase the time available both for incident-related work and proactive patrol.

Applying graded response

25. The control room is the hub of police operations, where many crucial deployment decisions are made. Control room operators play a key 'gatekeeping' role – to a significant degree, they determine what becomes police business. In the past, as the volume of incidents requiring police attention increased, forces adopted a policy of 'graded response'. This separates emergencies – which must be attended immediately – from incidents where a delayed response is appropriate, and deals in other ways with calls which do not require police attendance at all. The policy has helped forces deal more rationally with the thousands of calls they receive daily. But in some control rooms graded response is not being applied well, producing serious inefficiencies in the deployment of police officers and contributing to fire-brigade policing.

Grading of emergency calls

26. Contrary to popular perception, the main source of emergency calls is not the 999 line. Home Office research in four forces found that, on average, only 38 per cent of incidents requiring immediate response were reported by 999 call.[1] Moreover, although many people use the 999 system in good faith to report something which is not actually an emergency, there is, unfortunately, a degree of deliberate misuse of 999. The first decision that the control room operator makes after receiving a 999 or other call is whether the incident does merit immediate response – typically, where there is a crime in progress, a threat of violence or injury exists, or where a road accident has led to a major delay or congestion. By definition, these are serious incidents to which the police must always be ready to make the fastest response consistent with road safety. The volume per officer of such calls is a key determinant of decisions on minimum staffing levels and the organisation of resources, because immediate response vehicles are usually double-crewed. Thus, when operators over-grade calls by classifying them as emergencies when they fall outside the agreed criteria, they cause inefficiencies in deployment.

[1]
Around 42 per cent were reported on other telephone lines, and the remaining 20 per cent originated from various other sources such as police officers radioing in or from the fire brigade. (Lara Diez, *The Use of Call Grading*, Police Research Paper 13, Home Office, 1995.)

Exhibit 8
Variations in grading decisions, 1994/95

Some forces grade many more incidents as emergencies than other forces, despite similar definitions of an emergency.

Source: Audit Commission analysis of information from forces under the provisions of the Local Government Act 1992

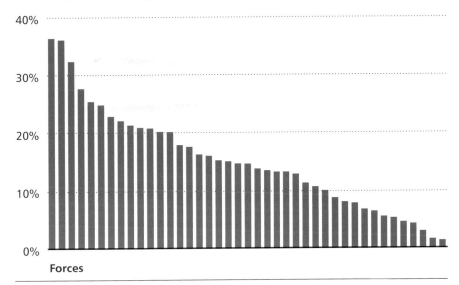

Percentage of incidents graded 'immediate response'

Forces

27. The variation between forces is significant (Exhibit 8). Several forces grade more than 30 per cent of calls as emergencies while, at the other extreme, one force gave this grade to just over 1 per cent of calls. In the five provincial fieldwork forces, the percentage of calls graded as emergencies varied less dramatically, from 12 to 31 per cent. The Home Office research on call grading found no relationship between these different percentages and the number or nature of incidents with which forces deal – principally, explanation lies in the operators' interpretation of the calls.

28. The activation of an intruder alarm is treated as an immediate response call because it may mean that a crime is in progress, but the vast majority are in fact false alarms. This is a particular concern to police managers seeking to make the best use of their officers' time, and ACPO recently reviewed its policy of attending alarms that repeatedly malfunction. In 1994, 1.1 million activations of remote-signalling intruder alarms were checked by the police, typically by a double-crewed response unit. Some 92 per cent of these activations – just over one million – were false alarms.[1] It takes between 15 and 40 minutes to check a false alarm and thus the minimum opportunity cost to the police was in the region of 500,000 hours. This translates into a financial cost of at least £13 million in 1994, which is a conservative sum. The provisions of the Police Act 1964 prevent forces from charging for attendance to alarms which persistently malfunction. Their only sanction is to downgrade the priority attached to that alarm call, or withdraw a police response altogether, but this is clearly unsatisfactory.

Police attendance at non-urgent incidents

29. There is also a variation, albeit less dramatic, in the number of incidents which are graded as non-urgent but still requiring a visit by a police officer (Exhibit 9, overleaf). Forces have less clear-cut criteria to guide operators in these decisions, and some retain a policy of trying to attend every reported

[1] Source: ACPO Intruder Alarm Working Group. Remote-signalling alarms are connected to commercial central stations, which contact the appropriate police force. In addition, there are estimated to be at least one million 'audible only' alarm activations to which police are often called, but on which no statistics are kept.

incident. In the fieldwork forces, the percentage of incidents attended varied from 67 to 91 per cent. In many cases, officers respond more promptly than the circumstances actually require; analysis in one local command unit revealed that officers were sent to 85 per cent of all reported incidents and typically arrived within 15 minutes. Not surprisingly, foot patrol officers rarely provided the first response. In another area, only 1 per cent of a sample of calls resulted in a scheduled appointment being made for later in the day or on the following day.

30. Different local circumstances will inevitably produce different attendance figures. But police officers are an expensive resource and their deployment should be subject to rational criteria, the implementation of which should be carefully monitored. The total number of incidents recorded by forces in 1994/95 was just over 19 million. One force is able to calculate that calls attended take 36 minutes on average from the dispatch of the officer to completion of work at the scene, excluding time spent on paperwork (Exhibit 10). In the absence of national data to the contrary, this suggests that each 10 per cent of calls to which officers are dispatched unnecessarily absorbs the equivalent nationally of around 700 officers. This is not time that is wasted as such, since both travelling to an incident and speaking to people on arrival raise police visibility, but it would otherwise be available for more proactive patrol. As forces have moved to larger control rooms covering several BCUs, local commanders have faced the dilemma that they are accountable for their

Exhibit 9
The percentage of incidents attended

In some basic command units the police attend all incidents; in others, less than 60 per cent.

Percentage of incidents attended by police officers

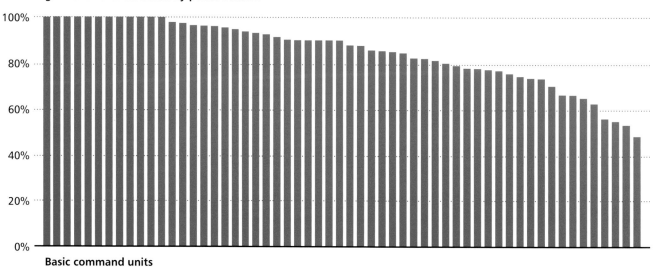

Basic command units

Source: Analysis of responses to a survey by the Audit Commission of aspects of patrol work in over 100 basic command units (BCUs) in English and Welsh provincial forces; it is referred to throughout this report as the BCU questionnaire. See Appendix 3 for details, and for a definition of BCUs.

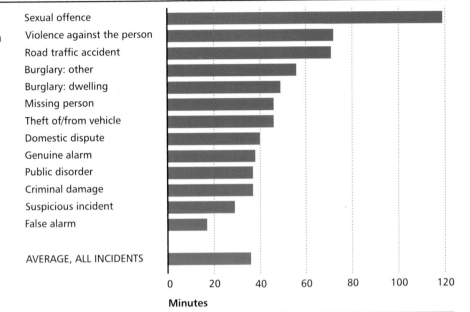

Exhibit 10
Time taken to deal with incidents in one force

The average elapsed time taken to deal with incidents is 36 minutes.

Source: Cleveland Constabulary's command and control system

Chart categories (top to bottom): Sexual offence, Violence against the person, Road traffic accident, Burglary: other, Burglary: dwelling, Missing person, Theft of/from vehicle, Domestic dispute, Genuine alarm, Public disorder, Criminal damage, Suspicious incident, False alarm, AVERAGE, ALL INCIDENTS

X-axis: Minutes (0, 20, 40, 60, 80, 100, 120)

use of resources but the main determinant of how patrol effort is expended – the control room – lies outside BCU command. (One solution has been to introduce service level agreements between control rooms and BCUs.)

31. Inconsistent decisions about attendance can also influence public perceptions of quality of service. In many forces, operators can refer calls about crimes to crime desk officers, who assess whether police attendance is likely to be fruitful. But for non-crime calls (up to 70 per cent of the total), control room staff have two options – to resolve the matter themselves or refer the call to a patrol officer. Under pressure, many choose the latter option even for relatively trivial incidents. Thus a person might report a stolen car and be dealt with by a crime desk officer over the telephone, while on the same day complain about inconsiderate parking and be visited by a police officer. This would send confusing signals about police priorities.

Supervision and monitoring in the control room

32. Clearly, control room staff should err on the side of caution in deciding whether to send a police officer in their attempt to provide the best service for the caller. But at times they fail to glean sufficient information from the caller to determine the most appropriate response – in effect, they act as simple dispatchers rather than controllers. This may be due to a combination of pressure to meet target times set by the force to pick up incoming calls, inadequate training (the average training in fieldwork forces was ten days) and a lack of supervision. In one fieldwork force, a control room where the post of supervisor had been abolished graded 41 per cent of a sample of calls as requiring immediate response. A busier, neighbouring area with a supervised control room gave this emergency grade to 22 per cent of calls.

Exhibit 11
Control room workload

There is a fivefold variation in workload between BCUs.

The number of incidents dealt with per control room operator per shift

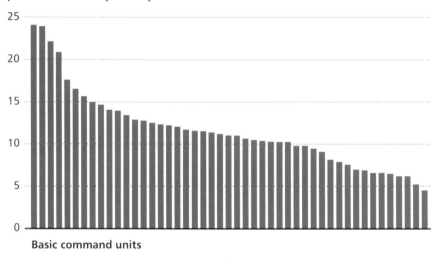

Basic command units

Source: Analysis of questionnaire returns from those BCUs able to provide this information

33. In some control rooms, the workload on operators restricts the time available to talk to callers; the number of incidents is a principal factor in workload and, again, considerable variations exist between different areas (Exhibit 11). Some of the calls relate to other agencies' services – utilities and local authorities, for example – which the police handle out of a commitment to quality of service. It is, however, questionable whether the burden is an appropriate one. Technology may also be a factor. If the force lacks a sufficient number of well-publicised, direct lines, or the telephone system does not have an efficient queuing or diversion system, operators will experience more pressure to deal with the flashing red lights of incoming calls.

34. Evaluation of control room performance – through control room supervisors, senior managers or internal inspectorates – is therefore essential if patrol officers are to be deployed efficiently, but some forces still do not monitor control room performance in this way. Patrol officers are also well placed to assess whether their attendance at incidents has been useful, but they are rarely asked in a systematic way for their perspective on control room decisions. The Commission surveyed patrol officers[1] to glean their views; 24 per cent were dissatisfied with the usual decisions about whether incidents merited police attendance, while 43 per cent felt that incorrect gradings had been applied. Although such judgements always benefit from hindsight, these figures suggest that a considerable gulf exists between the views of control room staff and patrol officers.

[1]
An Audit Commission questionnaire was completed by 490 patrol constables and sergeants in six fieldwork forces: see Appendix 3 for details of issues covered, methodology and response rate.

Matching resources to demand

35. Many forces have responded to rising workload by trying to put more officers on duty at times of peak demand. The traditional four-relief system has roughly the same numbers of officers on duty in the quiet hours and at the busiest times – usually 4pm through to late evening. Changes in regulations in 1993 enabled forces to introduce variable shift arrangements, although 60 per cent of officers on shifts still work the traditional system. However, the introduction of variable shifts has not completely resolved the mismatch with demand (Exhibit 12). Responses to the BCU questionnaire indicate that 16 per cent of operational patrol officers are on duty at 7pm, when workload is peaking, while 11 per cent are on duty during the quietest period, in the early hours of the morning. Almost one in ten BCUs had the most officers available for patrol at 5am. The mismatch between incidents and resources is explained in part by the practice of double-crewing patrol cars at night (for reasons of officer safety), although the pattern of double-crewing varies between, and sometimes within, forces.

36. Attempts to tackle these problems encounter two constraints. Firstly, considerations of officers' morale may preclude a shift system which requires them to work a greater number of 'late turns', typically 2pm to 10pm. Secondly, national conditions of service are laid down on matters such as the length of shifts and changes to work patterns which limit management's room for manoeuvre. In one force visited, managers sought to bring forward a shift starting and finishing time by 30 minutes. Although informal soundings showed that most staff favoured the proposal, it was dropped because of inflexibility in the national rules governing changes to working hours.

37. Problems in meeting demand efficiently can also flow from 'abstractions', when officers rostered for duty are not available due to planned absences such as training, leave and court attendance, or because of unplanned absences such as sickness. Returns to the BCU questionnaire show an average abstraction level in patrol sections of around 21 per cent, but in some BCUs the figure

Exhibit 12
Match of resources to demand

An optimal shift pattern would have more officers on duty from 4pm to 10pm than at present.

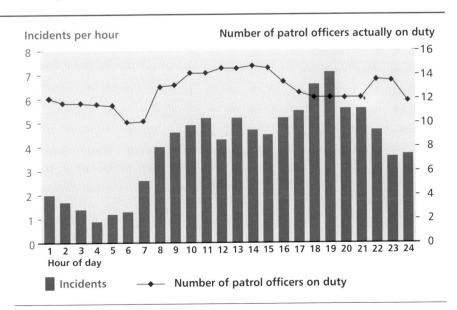

Source: Audit Commission analysis of data from a typical BCU in a fieldwork force

Exhibit 13
Sickness absence levels

There is a fourfold variation in levels of sickness absence.

Source: HMIC Matrix, 1994

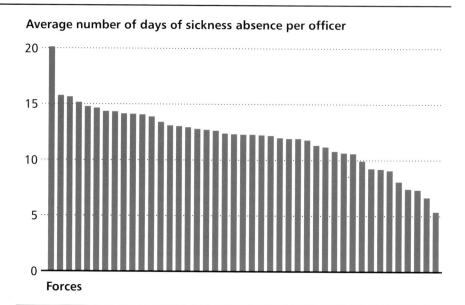

Average number of days of sickness absence per officer

Forces

approached 50 per cent on a snapshot day. Sickness absence is the principal cause of unplanned abstraction; it averages just over twelve days per year per officer, but there is a fourfold variation between forces (Exhibit 13). The variation cannot be explained by the type of force, as significant differences occur within metropolitan and largely rural forces. Patrol sections suffer more from abstraction than other parts of the force because they are the obvious reservoir of officers to call on whenever there is a special need. Around half the BCUs responding to the questionnaire set minimum staffing levels for patrol, to protect patrol strength, but in practice these are often not maintained. The recognised difficulties of forward planning are, on occasions, compounded by poor management of known abstractions (especially where IT is inadequate), and late calls for court attendance. Sergeants may not know until the shift starts how many officers are actually available for street duty.

The use of supplementary provision

38. Attention has so far focused on managing the initial response to calls for service and the way that patrol officers are deployed. But some police forces are missing opportunities offered by the Special Constabulary to help bridge the gap between supply and public demand for visible policing. Special Constables are civilian volunteers given full police powers by being sworn in before a magistrate. They perform a valuable role in boosting the visible police presence, especially at times of peak demand such as Friday and Saturday nights. There are currently about 20,000 such officers, with a wide variation between forces in their strength as a proportion of regular officer numbers – urban areas clearly find it harder to recruit volunteers (Exhibit 14). Although they receive only expenses, Specials are not a free resource – they must be trained, equipped and supervised, at an estimated annual cost per head of around £1,500. This represents substantial expenditure across the country, but some forces may not be getting the best from this resource.

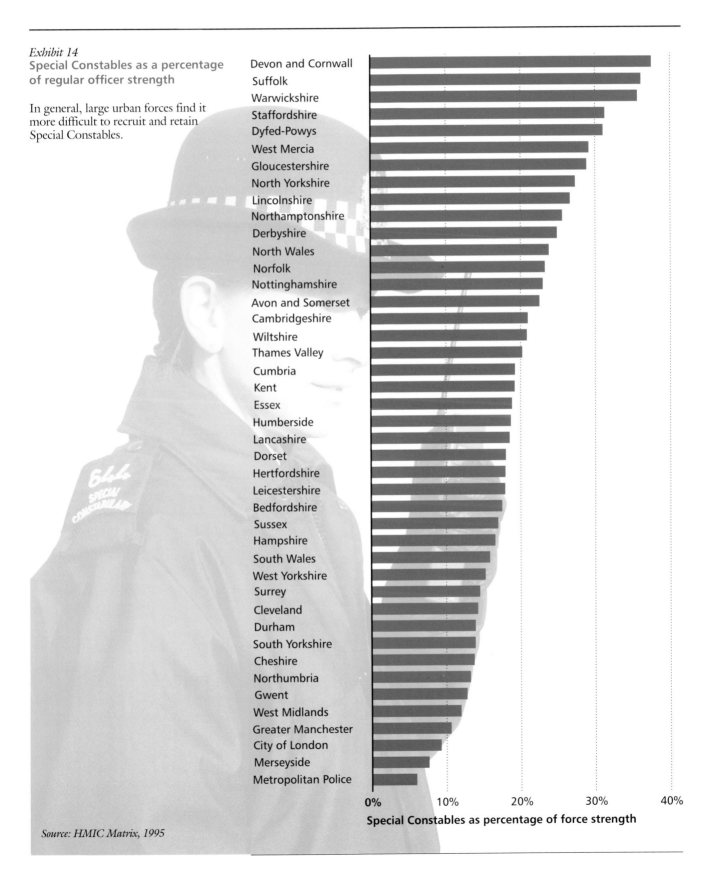

Exhibit 14
Special Constables as a percentage of regular officer strength

In general, large urban forces find it more difficult to recruit and retain Special Constables.

Devon and Cornwall
Suffolk
Warwickshire
Staffordshire
Dyfed-Powys
West Mercia
Gloucestershire
North Yorkshire
Lincolnshire
Northamptonshire
Derbyshire
North Wales
Norfolk
Nottinghamshire
Avon and Somerset
Cambridgeshire
Wiltshire
Thames Valley
Cumbria
Kent
Essex
Humberside
Lancashire
Dorset
Hertfordshire
Leicestershire
Bedfordshire
Sussex
Hampshire
South Wales
West Yorkshire
Surrey
Cleveland
Durham
South Yorkshire
Cheshire
Northumbria
Gwent
West Midlands
Greater Manchester
City of London
Merseyside
Metropolitan Police

0%   10%   20%   30%   40%

Special Constables as percentage of force strength

Source: HMIC Matrix, 1995

39. One reason why some forces are not maximising their use of Specials is that, according to the BCU questionnaire returns, the average duty commitment of Specials is four hours per week. Not surprisingly, most police supervisors view this as too short a period to merit assigning significant responsibilities to Specials. All forces use them for foot patrol, and 70 per cent also put them on mobile patrol duties, but few offer Specials the chance to develop their patrolling skills and take on more challenging duties. This could be one factor in the high turnover – around 25 per cent of Special Constables leave the service each year, and many stay for less than two years.[1] Some join the regular service or leave for unavoidable reasons, but a current review by the Home Office and ACPO is examining the problem to identify ways in which avoidable losses can be reduced.

40. Another principal source of support to police patrol is the contribution from other bodies with a role in community safety. The police service recognised many years ago that its own effectiveness depended in part on the calibre of working relationships with other agencies whose remit included crime and community safety – the courts, probation service, health agencies, business groups, the voluntary sector and, most importantly, local authorities. There is a network of partnership arrangements operating in even the smallest force that would take pages to document. The service has worked very hard to make a success of these arrangements, and there are many individual success stories to tell, but some police managers express concern that:

◆ too often, partnerships are an assortment of projects and ad hoc initiatives, lacking formal structures and a unifying sense of purpose;

◆ projects do not always have objectives and timescales; those objectives which are set may not accord with the broader plans of each partnership agency;

◆ talk may not be matched by action and concrete achievements;

◆ programmes are not subject to rigorous evaluation of benefits; and

◆ where forces' commitment to partnership working is not matched by other agencies, the police can find themselves substituting for other professionals rather than exploiting their expertise.

41. One result of the 'thin blue line' becoming thinner is that the private sector has sought to fill part of the vacuum left by declining foot patrol – there are now more people employed as security guards than there are police officers. However, there is increasing concern about the lack of public accountability of these private arrangements, and little evidence that security guards fulfil the public's need for reassurance. The reason may in part be the absence of statutory regulation, which has allowed some security firms to be set up by, and employ, people with convictions for theft and violence. Also, security guards are there to stop people doing things, usually stealing, rather than to help or reassure law-abiding citizens.

[1]
In contrast, the turnover of retained firefighters is just over 7 per cent per year.

42. The problems posed by public expectations are compounded by a trend of rising demand that shows little sign of abating. Both are factors over which the police can exercise only limited control but, as shown above, their response to the challenge can be hampered if there are shortcomings in managing this demand or in exploiting the additional contributions of Special Constables. Action to break out of the reactive pattern of policing and deal more efficiently with incidents will not in itself enable forces to reap all the benefits of effective patrol. They also need to ensure that officers use what time *is* available for proactive work to best effect.

4 Direction and Targeting of Patrol

Some forces are not using officers' non-incident time as productively as others, partly because they do not make it clear what they expect officers to achieve from patrol.

Where patrol effort is directed at the symptoms of problems rather than the underlying causes, officers' time is tied up in repeat visits.

Briefings are too variable in quality to provide a sufficient focus for proactive work. Debriefings are rare.

Beat work continues to have low status within forces, so good officers are lost to the beat. Supervision and tutoring may need to change to reflect new styles of patrol.

43. Getting the right number of officers on duty at the right time and reducing inappropriate responses to incidents are necessary but not sufficient conditions to reap the full benefits of effective patrol. Forces also need to ensure that non-incident time is used as productively as possible. This section reviews current practice against the following features of good practice:

◆ setting clear objectives so that officers know what patrol is meant to achieve; although outcomes are difficult to measure, it is important to evaluate the impact of patrol work and not just the volume of activity;

◆ avoiding a short-term focus that fails to get to the roots of problems;

◆ focusing briefings at the beginning of the shift on high-quality, local intelligence; encouraging debriefings and raising the profile of intelligence work;

◆ striving to raise the status of beat work; and

◆ ensuring that tutoring and supervision lead to efficient use of officers' time.

Objectives for patrol

44. Many officers are unclear what proactive patrol is meant to accomplish, other than unquantifiable reassurance. This may be due to only partial success in cascading force goals, or because local objectives are not framed in ways which help officers focus their day-to-day efforts. Patrol constables in fieldwork forces were asked about their awareness of, and involvement in, setting objectives at both the force and local level. The results suggest that, despite recent improvements in planning processes,[1] further work is needed on consultation and the communication of operational objectives (Table 2, overleaf). Advocates of bottom-up planning will be disappointed that, if the fieldwork forces are typical, less than a third of patrol constables have been consulted on local priorities, and only 7 per cent on force objectives.

45. In addition to the objectives and priorities agreed at force and local level, all forces must now have regard to the Home Secretary's key objectives, one of which is 'to provide high visibility policing so as to reassure the public'. The high profile given to reassurance patrol accords with public expectations, but for all of the reasons cited earlier it is a difficult objective to achieve. Many forces have not yet worked systematically through four key steps:

◆ how are we defining 'high visibility'?

◆ have we identified target locations and times for intensive patrol effort?

◆ *how* have these been identified – are they based on crime hot spots, concentrations of people such as in town centres during rush hour, or on the needs of particularly vulnerable groups such as crime victims or pensioners?

◆ is achievement of high visibility, reassurance patrol effort being monitored?

[1]
See the Audit Commission's report, *Cheques and Balances: a Management Handbook on Police Planning and Financial Delegation*, HMSO, 1994, for a fuller consideration of police planning processes.

Table 2
Patrol constables' involvement in setting objectives

Percentage of constables who are:	Fieldwork forces						
	A	B	C	D	E	F	Average
Consulted on force objectives	7%	12%	2%	8%	6%	7%	7%
Consulted on local objectives	38%	40%	15%	18%	36%	24%	29%
Fully aware of local objectives	46%	40%	32%	26%	44%	35%	37%
Influenced by local objectives in their patrol work	26%	46%	26%	27%	27%	29%	29%
Involved in planning initiatives to tackle local problems	73%	58%	47%	43%	51%	59%	55%

Source: Audit Commission survey of 409 patrol constables in six fieldwork forces

The difficulty of measuring patrol outcomes

46. Posing this last question would currently produce the answer 'no' in most forces. Many areas of police work are subject to a battery of performance indicators which attempt to measure efficiency and effectiveness: patrol, however, is not one of them. Of the suite of 25 national indicators currently monitored by the Audit Commission, HMIC, ACPO and the Home Office, only two relate to preventive or reassurance patrol. These capture the amount of time spent working in public by constables, and public satisfaction with levels of foot and mobile patrol. The latter may, however, reflect factors other than effective patrol effort. The difficulty in gauging successful outcomes of patrol work stems partly from the lack of clear objectives; without these, forces are ill-equipped to analyse the links between what their officers hope to accomplish and what they spend their time doing.

47. Another difficulty is that effective intervention by patrol officers based on informal resolution, rather than enforcement, is often not captured in a quantifiable way. This can be illustrated using an example of effective problem-solving from one force visited (Box B). The arrests or cautions which followed repeated visits by patrol officers dispatched to deal with disturbances at one address were recorded, but the action by the inspector that finally resolved the problem was not. A monitoring system that gauges effectiveness only through conventional statistics could therefore undermine rather than reinforce a problem-solving approach, the essence of which is to identify and eradicate causes.

Symptoms rather than causes – the short-term focus of patrol work

48. The successful outcome described in Box B highlights both a strength and a weakness of current patrol work – though the capacity to intervene and resolve recurring problems through analysis and local knowledge exists, this approach is more the exception than the rule. Police work will always have a significant element of reactivity – incidents are the core business. But the response is less effective if patrol officers approach these incidents not as problems to be resolved, but rather as one-off events that need 'sorting'. Then, the symptoms of a problem receive their attention but not the cause. Thus officers may routinely damp down a disturbance but not explore the factors that led to it; or disperse a group of unruly youths without feeling much obligation to consider how future anti-social behaviour by the same group in the same location might be prevented. Failure to get to the root of the problem first time out means that resources are more likely to be absorbed in repeat visits.

49. There are a number of reasons why problem-solving occurs on an ad hoc rather than systematic basis:

♦ many forces struggle with poor information systems that make it hard for officers to discern the relationships between incidents;

♦ patrol sections lack the analytical facility to interrogate what information does exist so that problems can be correctly identified and solutions devised;

♦ there is an unwillingness on the part of some patrol officers to take ownership of underlying problems, mainly due to the way that duties are assigned;

♦ the prevailing organisational culture is not one that invests the time and management support needed for this style of policing to flourish. Unless a problem-solving approach is ingrained as everyday practice, it will wither on the vine in the face of constant pressure simply to react.

Information and analysis needed for problem-solving

50. The starting point for a problem-solving approach is to analyse systematically calls for service. Recent improvements in the investigation of crime are based on information and intelligence systems that focus attention on patterns of crimes, rather than seeing them as isolated incidents. In a few

---

Box B
Informal solutions are hard to measure

Source: Northumbria Police

An inspector leading a community policing team was concerned about the repeated call-outs to deal with disorder and fighting at a particular address almost every Friday night, absorbing officers' time both in restoring order and dealing with the aftermath if arrests were made. On visiting, he realised the problem was a severe clash of personalities between two neighbours, which often erupted into violence when one or both men had been drinking. He spoke to the local housing officer, who offered one of the families a move to another part of the estate, which was accepted gratefully. No more police attention was required at either address. However, although the arrests and cautions from earlier attendances were recorded in statistics, the successful intervention by the inspector was not.

forces this approach has been extended to non-crime work, which lends itself to similar analysis of trends, patterns, repeat locations, multiple offenders and repeat complainants. But overall, patrol work has not benefited from investment in analytical approaches or technical support. Consequently, managers lack real-time information to help them target patrol effort on crime and disorder hot spots. The recent success of the New York Police Department in reducing crime is attributed in large part to the use of computer-generated analysis of hot spots.

'...patrol work has not benefited from investment in analytical approaches or technical support.'

51. In fact, American research[I] suggests that nuisance and disorder incidents are not evenly distributed; 64 per cent of calls to police originated from just 5 per cent of addresses. Although the research has not been repeated in this country, the American experience accords with officers' experience here. Every officer knows that a few high-profile locations pose chronic problems, but less obvious repeat ones escape attention. Thus, although police are called again and again to the same addresses, the absence of analysis means that they are not fully aware of patterns that would highlight the need for long-term solutions. As yet, less than one in five forces has an information system with the capacity to identify repeat victims or locations – but not all of these actually use this facility to direct patrol activity.

52. These deficiencies mean that officers are routinely dispatched to incidents when they lack vital pieces of information which would help them deal satisfactorily with the situation they will encounter. For example, 90 per cent of known domestic violence involves systematic, repeated assault.[II] Yet many officers interviewed during fieldwork commented that they regularly attend domestic violence incidents without accurate, up-to-date information on previous assaults, whether charges had been brought, whether an injunction is in force against one of the partners, if there are children likely to be present or on the at-risk register – vital information to make sound decisions and take positive action at the scene.

Local identification and ownership

53. Deficiencies in the information and analysis needed to support a problem-solving approach are exacerbated by the fact that, until recently, most forces did not organise patrol duties in such a way as to encourage officers to identify with a particular area and take ownership of the policing problems that occur there. Traditionally, patrol assignments were based on time of day – officers were grouped into four shifts, or reliefs, responsible for policing a whole BCU or sub-division for an eight-hour period. At the end of that period, responsibility and problems could be handed over to the next shift. No-one below the chief inspector (operations) and the BCU commander held total responsibility for patrol across the whole geographic area, and these officers were too removed from day-to-day activities to be effective problem-solvers. Although forces are increasingly organising patrol work to extend geographical responsibilities, and thus ownership of problems, elements of the traditional approach remain in parts of many forces. Typically, 15 per

I
See, for example, Sherman et al, 'Hot Spots and Predatory Crime: Routine Activities and the Criminology of Place', *Criminology*, Vol. 27 pp27-55 (based on research in Minneapolis).

II
Morley and Mullender, *Preventing Domestic Violence to Women*, Police Research Group Paper No. 48, Home Office, 1994.

cent of patrol constables have a long-term assignment to a particular area, with some discretion to set their own working hours.

54. The traditional basis of duty assignment militates against officers acquiring in-depth knowledge of particular areas and their inhabitants. Such local knowledge contributes to effective intelligence-gathering, and is much valued by the public on the grounds that the officer is more likely to spot when something or someone is out of place. In theory, all patrol work is organised around beats. However, in practice, police managers tend to assign patrol officers on reliefs first to response duties – crewing either fast-response or 'panda' cars covering a large area. Any remaining officers are assigned to beats (Exhibit 15), but not necessarily to the same ones each time. Even where officers are given a beat to patrol, demands across the whole command area reduce the amount of time they are able to spend on that beat. Some spend more than half of their patrol time working in other areas.

Exhibit 15
Beat policing

Up to two-thirds of patrol constables are assigned to a specific beat at the start of their shift.

Percentage of patrol constables given a specific beat to patrol

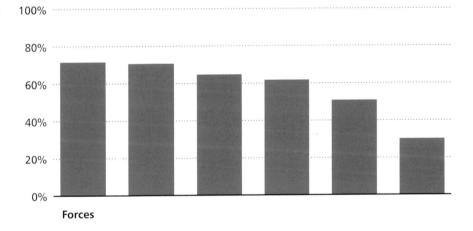

Forces

Source: Audit Commission survey of 409 patrol constables in fieldwork forces

Briefing and debriefing of patrol officers

55. A potential mechanism for communicating what the force is trying to achieve, and for focusing officers' efforts on local problems, is the briefing session at the beginning of each shift. It can also be a means of promoting *esprit de corps* – often the first ten minutes of the shift is the only time that all officers meet together. Although briefings should form an important link between strategy and operational activity, they often fail to do so because of shortcomings in their style and content, namely:

◆ inadequate preparation leads to a lack of focus – it is asking a lot of sergeants that they should prepare the briefing in their own time, although many do so;

◆ some briefings contain too many items, and thus lose officers' attention, especially if the information is not specific to the beat or BCU area;

◆ direct input from intelligence officers is occasional, that from CID officers even rarer. Briefings are too often one-way flows of information *to* PCs rather than an exchange of information and ideas;

◆ briefings are usually informal, which may be a problem if the informality fails to set an appropriate pace for the day's agenda;

◆ some rooms used for briefings are cluttered and noisy and prone to interruption during the briefing – not an arrangement conducive to good communication.

56. Even more problematic than poor briefings is the absence in most forces of effective debriefing. Only 5 per cent of patrol officers interviewed stated that they were systematically debriefed by their sergeants, which means that valuable information-sharing and learning opportunities are being lost. There are practical difficulties, especially when shifts do not overlap – bringing officers together for a debriefing would denude cover on the streets. But even where shift overlaps offer scope for structured briefing and debriefing sessions, the opportunity is often missed.

57. One consequence of inadequate briefing and debriefing is a reduced commitment to gathering and sharing intelligence. One in four patrol officers responding to the Commission's survey had not submitted any intelligence items in the previous seven tours of duty; just under 40 per cent had submitted three or more items in the same period. Responses to the BCU questionnaire also revealed considerable variations (Exhibit 16). Although quantity does not matter above quality, some Local Intelligence Officers are being starved of the raw data needed to construct quality indices on local criminals and their habits; there is evidence that patrol officers also believe that not enough intelligence is being collected and disseminated.[1]

58. As a result of these weaknesses, constables lack direction in how to use the time not absorbed by incidents. Unless they have been assiduous in briefing themselves, or the force has succeeded in cascading strategic objectives to the level of individual officers, many officers will default to doing what interests them or what *they* consider to be important. This may be neither foot patrol,

[1]
In May 1995 the Police Federation surveyed its members and analysed over 73,000 returns; 91 per cent of respondents said that *more* information, including intelligence, would improve the results of police patrol work, and 95 per cent cited the need for better quality intelligence.

Exhibit 16
Intelligence gathering by patrol officers

Some patrol officers gather far more intelligence than others.

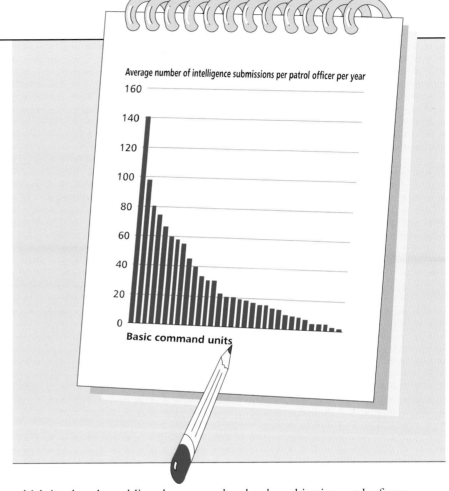

Average number of intelligence submissions per patrol officer per year

Basic command units

Source: Analysis of questionnaire returns from those BCUs able to provide this information

which is what the public values, nor related to key objectives set by force managers. It is more likely to be oriented towards traffic offences (for example, defective vehicles or disqualified drivers) or alternatively the officer will drive around in response mode, waiting for the call to the next job. Such discretion may have been appropriate in the past, but is likely to be problematic in an era of much more formal accountability through Local Policing Plans and key performance indicators.

The status of beat work

59. One antidote to fire-brigade policing, with its emphasis on short-term responses, is to create a climate in which managing a beat – developing local knowledge and contacts to tackle effectively a range of policing problems – is an attractive proposition for skilled and experienced officers. Some forces have worked very hard, and with marked success, to endow beat management with a higher status. But in many areas such efforts falter because of deeply ingrained attitudes that undervalue this type of proactive patrol work. The Commission's survey of patrol officers found that only 30 per cent believe that their forces value patrol as very important work.

'...working a beat is close to the bottom rung of the police status ladder...'

60. In contrast to the very high esteem in which patrol officers are held by the public, working a beat is close to the bottom rung of the police status ladder and is widely regarded as an unpopular posting. Some of the reasons for this attitude are obvious but hard to resolve. For example, patrol duty necessarily involves shift working, which can be stressful and disruptive to family or social routines. Working outdoors is clearly more physically demanding than a desk job, and patrol officers face potentially dangerous situations when responding to some incidents – in 1994, more than 15,000 police officers were assaulted on duty. Another factor is that while patrol is often described as the most important job in policing it is also, perhaps paradoxically, where all new recruits begin work.

61. Other factors contributing to the problems of low status and unpopularity relate to prevailing attitudes towards patrol work, present in all ranks, that could be more effectively challenged by senior officers, who often assert that this is the most important role in policing. Patrol officers often perceive themselves to be at the back of the queue when new equipment, such as cars and radios, is allocated, and that their needs for uniform upgrades such as high-quality waterproof jackets are not given a high priority. Facilities are relatively poor in many stations – for example, constables lack quiet spaces for writing reports. Particularly damaging is the fact that a move to any specialist post is viewed as an upward step, even when the rank is unchanged. Conversely, the threat of being sent back on the streets is held over the heads of CID or other specialist officers who are under-performing. Beat work is usually seen as a stepping-stone to more rewarding work rather than a specialism in its own right, and there are few incentives, financial or otherwise, for good patrol officers to stay on the beat.

Supervising patrol

62. This perception that patrol work is not a specialism is, to independent observers, not entirely rational. It has long been recognised by researchers and commentators that patrol work can be complex and at times requires levels of expertise and interpersonal skills that test the qualities of even the most experienced officers. For example:

◆ patrol officers are usually first at the scene of a crime or serious incident – their actions can either lay the foundations for success or jeopardise subsequent investigation;

◆ patrol officers are a principal point of contact with members of the public, and their actions and conduct do much to shape overall perceptions of the police;

◆ patrol officers are often required to make instant decisions, under pressure, as to whether an arrestable offence has been committed – public order law, in particular, is difficult to interpret.

63. These features highlight the need not only for a high level of skill on the part of patrol officers but also for effective supervision. And yet patrol officers, with the exception of inexperienced probationers, are subject to less direct supervision or subsequent inspection of their actions than most other officers.

Clearly, over-the-shoulder supervision by sergeants is unwarranted. Progressive police management styles now emphasise a different role – that of a team leader who is both mentor and motivator. Not all sergeants have made this transition successfully. In some cases they are still awaiting appropriate training, but many are still operating within a conventional framework which is not well geared to the team approach. Supervision may be focused too much on the indirect products of patrol, such as files and other paperwork, with insufficient attention paid to the work carried out on the streets.

64. Contact between constables and sergeants is relatively limited once shift briefings are over. Activity sampling shows that, on average, 14 per cent of sergeants' time is accounted for by direct supervision; constables are not usually accompanied on patrol by their sergeants. Responses to the Commission's patrol constable survey indicate that less than half were given any tasks by their sergeant in their last tour of duty; one in six said that the sergeant determined how non-incident time was spent; and officers were four times more likely to decide themselves what activities they undertook than be guided by their sergeant (Exhibit 17).

Exhibit 17
Who determines how patrol constables spend their time?

Sergeants give constables little direction on how to spend their time.

Percentage of patrol constables' activities initiated by...

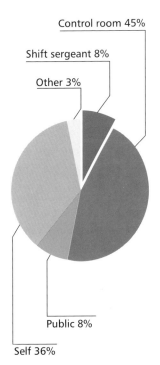

Control room 45%

Shift sergeant 8%

Other 3%

Public 8%

Self 36%

Use of non-incident time is determined by...

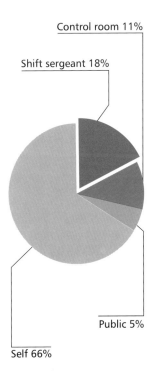

Control room 11%

Shift sergeant 18%

Public 5%

Self 66%

Source: Audit Commission survey of 409 patrol constables in six fieldwork forces

Tutoring of probationers

65. Although raw recruits to the service are obviously subject to much more direct supervision, any weaknesses in their training will have a disproportionate impact on patrol work. This is because a significant element of patrol, particularly in urban areas, is carried out by probationers ie, officers with less than two years service. On occasion, foot patrol is done *only* by probationers, because all other officers are assigned to cars to provide rapid response. Replies to the Commission's questionnaire to BCUs indicate that, on average, probationers comprise 17 per cent, but in some areas 30 per cent, of the core patrol strength. How well prepared are they for this role?

66. During their first seven months in the service, new officers complete a modular training programme that includes 15 weeks at a regional training centre and in-force training. This is shorter than the initial training received in other European forces – for example, recruits to the French gendarmerie attend a police academy for 12 months, German police officers for 18 months – but the probationers interviewed for this study felt that their training equipped them well for patrol. Each probationer is assigned to an experienced constable for on-the-job tutoring during the first seven months, at the end of which successful officers are declared 'fit for independent patrol', gaining the skills needed for full constable duties over the remainder of the two-year probation period.

67. Although many probationers learn a lot from their tutors, few forces have robust selection criteria for, and formal evaluation of, tutoring. This can mean that weaknesses are not exposed. For example, one probationer interviewed was very dissatisfied with the assigned tutor, who exhibited the worst attributes of 'canteen culture', but felt powerless to seek redress without being singled out as difficult. Another officer coming to the end of the two-year probation period had never been out on foot patrol with her tutor, thus limiting her ability to pick up beatcraft skills. Training Support at Harrogate, which co-ordinates the formal aspects of probationer training, favours the assignment of probationers not to ordinary shift duties but to dedicated training units. Here, a small group works as a team under the close supervision of a tutor constable. However, this approach may be feasible only in larger forces where there are sufficient numbers of probationers, and around two-thirds of BCUs report that probationers are still assigned to shifts.

'Forces are at a crossroads.'

68. The problems described above are not insoluble, but they require both careful analysis and appropriate action. Forces are at a crossroads. The changing nature of society has increased the volume and range of demands that the public makes on the police. Each force needs to take stock of its current approach to patrolling and consider whether it could improve levels of foot patrol, the grading of calls and the use of information to support and direct patrol. Some forces are already well down the road towards a proactive, problem-solving style of policing, which attempts to strengthen the capacity of communities to maintain high standards of order and neighbourliness. The next chapter identifies actions to help others to take the same route.

By managing resources better and targeting patrol effort, police forces could meet demand from the public more effectively.

But action is also required by the Home Office and others to shape public expectations and strengthen multi-agency partnerships. Forces can also improve their links with local communities.

The police cannot do it all – the route to safer communities involves other agencies and other approaches, such as CCTV.

The agenda for change is substantial but achievable; the prize for success is a strengthening of 'policing by consent'.

5   Police Patrol – the Way Forward

69. Many chief officers believe that rising demand must be met by increasing police resources. However, the decision on what share of total public expenditure should be allocated to policing is a political one and thus falls outside the scope of this report. The main question posed at the outset of this study was: are police forces making the best use of the resources already available to them in respect of patrol? The analysis summarised in earlier chapters suggests that good practice is not universal, and action is needed to meet public demand more effectively through better management of that demand and more targeted patrol effort (Exhibit 18). The benefits of effective patrol – patrol which has clear objectives, is intelligence-based, and responds to the problems that most disturb communities – make such action a high priority. It can help forces achieve a style of policing which treats communities as active partners in promoting reassurance and public safety. But action is needed not just by police forces. The Home Office and police authorities could shape public expectations so that they do not run too far ahead of what the police can deliver, and should seek to strengthen community safety partnerships.

Action by the Home Office and police authorities

70. Shaping public expectations is an essential task for the Home Office and police authorities. It requires frankness about what cannot be delivered and, where that is deemed unacceptable, a debate about resources and priorities. The Home Office could also help reduce inappropriate use of the 999 system through the kind of public information campaign that is being launched to influence expectations of out-of-hours calls to family doctors.

71. To succeed in shaping expectations police authorities, together with forces, need to get closer to communities and improve their means of consulting local people. Surveys of victims and users have helped forces to become more in tune with these expectations. Surveys could be even more valuable if there was a common methodology which would enable comparisons between results in different areas, thus helping forces to learn from others' successes.

'Shaping public expectations is an essential task...'

72. Forces are experimenting with other, more innovative approaches. Surrey, for example, is piloting a consumer panel – a cross-section of the community totalling some 400 individuals with whom information on policing issues is shared at regular intervals. In partnership with the Regional Council, Central Scotland Police uses a technique known as priority search, whereby professional facilitators work with local people to design a survey of public needs and priorities which asks questions from the viewpoint of service users, rather than providers. The results have fed directly into community safety policies drawn up jointly by the council and the police force.

73. Getting closer to communities also means giving relevant information *to* citizens so they know what service they can expect to receive, whether they are seeking or offering information, or reporting a crime or nuisance. In dealing with other service organisations, consumers increasingly negotiate a response and know what to expect – often an appointment for an agreed time. Similar principles should apply to policing. The rising volume of calls for service together with improvements in telecommunications mean that police forces

Exhibit 18
Problems, causes and solutions

There are three major reasons why the police are unable to fulfil public expectations of patrol, especially foot patrol.

PROBLEMS	CAUSES	ACTION	SOLUTIONS
Public expectations are not wholly realistic and exceed what the police can deliver.	The public is unclear about which matters are best dealt with by the police, and the standards of service it can expect to receive. Time available for preventive patrol is squeezed by incident response.		Shape expectations and inform the public about the service standards it can anticipate; target patrol effort in key locations for high visibility; make better use of supplementary provision (eg, Specials).
Many forces are not managing demand as well as they could; incidents dominate officers' attention.	Graded response is not being applied well. Officers are sent to jobs that do not merit police attendance. Many officers still work a traditional shift system that does not reflect patterns of demand; national conditions of service are a constraint on flexibility. Patrol sections suffer heavily from abstractions.		Improve training and supervision of control room staff; monitor application of graded response. Consider help desks; set criteria for officer attendance. Review national regulations on shift systems. Set and monitor target levels of patrol staffing.
Time available between incidents is not used as effectively as it could be.	What patrol is meant to achieve is not clear, thus it is difficult to set meaningful PIs. Forces lack analytical and problem-solving skills and adequate management information. Some briefings are poor and debriefings are rare; there is not enough detailed tasking/targeting. Patrol work has low status, thus there is little incentive for good officers to stay on the beat. Training in teambuilding is inadequate; belief in autonomy of constable blurs supervisory role.		Set clear objectives for patrol work; define achievable tasks and targets; monitor these and publicise success. Improve the quality of management information and analysis; ensure that problem-solving approaches are supported; assign more geographic responsibilities. Improve briefing and debriefing; set standards for intelligence submissions. Consider accreditation for beat manager role; improve working conditions for patrol officers. Supervise the process of patrol; encourage sergeants and inspectors to set leadership examples on the streets; quality assure the work of tutors.

Source: Audit Commission

deal with ever more issues over the telephone, even the investigation of crimes. On the evidence of public and victim surveys, the public accepts this[I] but the police can do more to influence expectations and dispel the illusion that they have limitless resources to meet every kind of need, day and night. Except in cases of real emergency, rapid response is less important than establishing clear expectations about response and then meeting them.

74. Local Policing Plans, spelling out local objectives and standards of service, can act as a bridge between the police and the community, so long as channels of communication are good. Ideally, these Plans reflect a consensus, which means resolving the potential dissonance between police priorities and the importance attached by the public to the diverse range of problems brought to police attention. Forces need, in particular, to formulate efficient and effective responses to anti-social behaviour and nuisance, to ensure that they address priorities across the full spectrum of community safety as well as the more obvious problems of serious crime. Such responses should be based on close analysis of this category of calls, together with clarification of where responsibilities lie.

Community safety – putting patrol in context

75. This emphasis on community safety is an important one. The reason why people want to see more police officers patrolling the streets is not because they find the sight aesthetically pleasing but because the streets are perceived as increasingly unsafe, and this perception diminishes people's quality of life. Patrolling officers do help to make the streets safer, but at any one time there is only one officer on the streets for every 8,000 citizens, and thus patrols alone cannot provide the degree of neighbourhood safety and personal reassurance that some would see as the ideal. Consequently, the police try to convey the message that bobbies on the beat are but one element of an effective, across-the-board policing strategy. They need more support from politicians – who often promote more foot patrol as a panacea for all ills – in communicating this message.

76. Because the police cannot do it all there is an increasing need for co-ordinated action by the police and other agencies. To secure this, it may be necessary for the Government to clarify the responsibilities of various agencies, notably but not solely local authorities, and set these within a statutory framework.[II] The essential role of other agencies is illustrated by the findings of the Central Scotland survey of local communities' needs. Only one demand – a visible police presence to reassure and deter anti-social behaviour – is solely a police responsibility. The others fall squarely within the remit of the local authority and other agencies: education on drug and alcohol abuse, improved street lighting, safer play areas, more leisure facilities, road safety measures, and attention to environmental concerns such as dogs fouling pavements and parks. The Commission's own survey confirmed the importance of inputs to community safety from agencies other than the police. It also identified another desired contribution to safer neighbourhoods – responsible parenting, producing a more disciplined attitude among children and young adults (Exhibit 19). The constable is clearly valued as representing a legitimate authority that many people feel is missing in the home and at school.

I

A recent example is the public survey carried out by Hampshire Constabulary. Callers were very satisfied if they were told whether, and if so when, police officers were likely to arrive and the officers then appeared at the appointed time.

II

A case for a statutory framework was made in *Safer Communities: The Local Delivery of Crime Prevention through the Partnership Approach* (the 'Morgan Report'), Home Office, 1991, but not accepted by the Government. The Commission will examine community safety issues in a future study.

Exhibit 19
The public's priorities for improving community safety

More responsible parenting is the top priority.

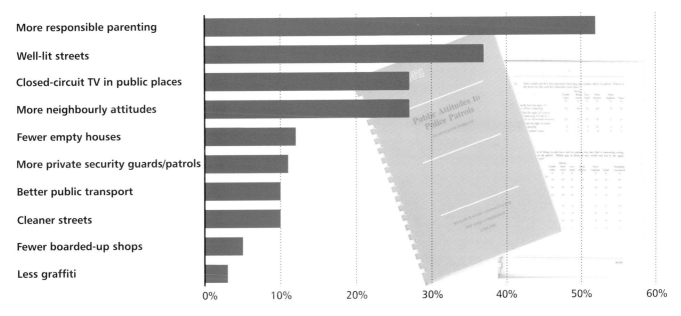

Percentage of survey respondents selecting this improvement

Note: Survey respondents were asked to select, from a list of ten possibilities, two or three changes other than more police on the beat that would make their neighbourhoods safer.

Source: Survey of 800 people conducted by MORI on behalf of the Audit Commission

77. One way of giving practical effect to the partnership approach would be to consider lifting from police control rooms the burden of answering queries about services provided by local authorities, health bodies, utilities and other agencies. As public sector services have become more fragmented, so the police have often become the first port of call for information and assistance. This burden could be shared more equitably if multi-agency information services were set up, possibly with funding supported by central government as part of its Citizen's Charter commitment to accessibility of services. Perhaps a 333 or similar number, publicised in the way that 999 is at present, could be adopted to maximise awareness and ease of use.

78. Action is also merited on burglar alarms, where the police service is in effect paying for inefficiencies in installation and maintenance. Compared with most European forces, the British police are unusual in providing the main initial response to burglar alarms. Public expectations may dictate that this remains the case but consideration should be given to allowing police forces to charge for attending persistently false alarms – a measure not primarily intended to generate income but to reduce the waste of police time. Alarm owners would then have a financial incentive to take appropriate steps, such as improving maintenance schedules or, in the case of businesses, adopting the American practice of installing cameras to give visual confirmation of break-in.

Action by police forces – spreading good practice

79. The police have much to gain from a better alignment between public expectations and what they can actually deliver. But the service should go further and take steps to break out of the current highly reactive pattern of activity, which stifles officers' ability to identify with local areas and reduces their willingness to take ownership of problems. Some forces have made great efforts to create the conditions necessary for a proactive style of patrol which meets the policing needs of the 1990s (Exhibit 20). These good practices tend to evolve gradually, so overnight change cannot be expected, but all forces now need to adopt the approaches already evident in some and:

◆ make graded response work, assessing emergencies more accurately and screening incidents that do not require police attendance, without alienating public support;

Exhibit 20
Making time for proactive work

Forces can create more time for proactivity by making graded response work well and managing resources more effectively.

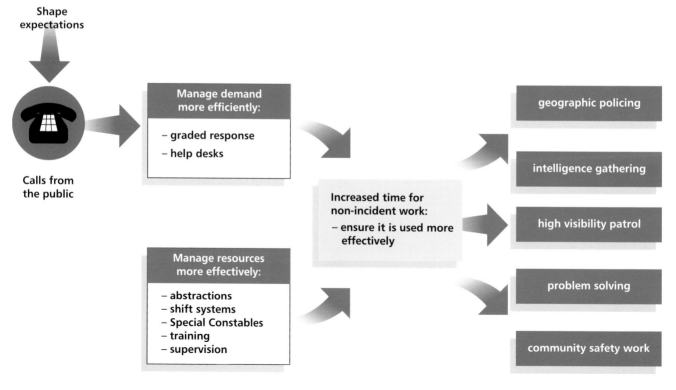

Source: Audit Commission

◆ match operational patrol resources more closely to demand;

◆ use analysis of demand to target patrol work and direct officer effort at the causes of problems rather than their symptoms;

◆ organise more patrol work on a geographic basis;

◆ raise the status of patrol work, and ensure that supervision is geared to new styles of patrol work – participative, team-based and problem-solving.

Managing demand – making graded response work

80. A starting point for change is the initial response to incidents – the police should not strive to supply a Rolls-Royce response where a more modest one would do. Calls should not be graded as emergencies when they do not require an emergency response, and officers should not be sent to incidents which do not merit attendance. Seeking to negotiate a greater number of delayed responses, preferably based on appointments, would help, as would planned improvements in control room technology. However, unless working practices are efficient, computerisation may simply mean that bad decisions are made more quickly. All forces therefore need to review, and where necessary revise, their:

◆ criteria for guiding decisions about graded response;

◆ mechanisms for supervising and monitoring implementation of this guidance;

◆ training programmes for control room staff; and

◆ ways of dealing with non-emergency calls that are not routed to crime desks.

81. Although each force sets its own criteria to determine whether an incident merits immediate response, there is much consistency of definition across the country. This offers scope for training packages to be produced nationally, spreading best practice and offering economies of scale. In the absence of such a package, many forces have developed their own training materials – Devon and Cornwall, for example, uses a self-assessment manual for its operators which has proved very helpful. However the criteria for grading incidents are defined, it is essential that they be well publicised, both internally and externally. Forces are now required to publish performance data on handling 999 calls and responding to emergencies. Many have taken the opportunity to explain what counts as an emergency – further avenues to raise public awareness should be explored.

82. Because of operators' natural tendency to adopt a 'just in case' approach, managers need to create a control room environment in which staff have time to talk to callers, are given feedback on their decisions and are not punished for errors of judgement made in good faith. Otherwise, operators will continue to work within the prevailing culture of near-automatic dispatch, with the main objective being to clear their screens by the end of the shift. Systematic monitoring should therefore be undertaken to review:

◆ the percentage of calls graded as emergencies and delayed responses, compared with a force or area profile of the expected pattern of grading;

◆ variation between operators in patterns of grading decisions;

◆ compliance with graded response, gauged by dip-sampling control room tapes, which also allows supervisors to check the overall quality of service given to the caller;

◆ the volume of calls per operator, profiled across 24-hour periods; and

◆ satisfaction of callers with the response provided, assessed by surveys.

The impact of this monitoring would be greater if forces could get feedback from patrol officers about grading decisions, and bring together control room staff to share experiences and learn from each other. BCU commanders should also monitor, and where necessary revise, the pattern of deployment of their officers.

83. The value of monitoring is illustrated by Thames Valley Police. Concerned at the high level of immediate responses, the force reviewed its grading criteria and then monitored how well control room staff were implementing the revised policy. In 1992, 38 per cent of calls were graded as emergencies; by 1994 this figure was down to 12 per cent. Because emergency responses are normally double-crewed, this released around 12,500 days – equivalent to 60 officers – for proactive work.

84. Scrutiny of control room practices may well reveal training needs. The police service rightly puts a high premium on training to ensure a skilled workforce, and forces need to ensure that civilian staff benefit appropriately from this investment in training. Thames Valley has recently extended its training course for control room staff to five weeks; this compares with an average of two weeks in the five provincial fieldwork forces. All forces should consider the practice, adopted by a few forces, whereby control room staff accompany officers on patrol at regular intervals. The Metropolitan Police also uses scenario training, exposing operators to a range of calls based on real events during which instructors are on hand to advise.

Help desks

85. In most control rooms, two categories of call are relatively straightforward to resolve; officers are automatically sent to emergencies, while crime calls are referred to crime desks to assess what action should follow. The focus for efficiency gains lies in the residual bulk of calls, up to 65 per cent, where the operator has discretion to decide if police attendance is appropriate; some forces have made great strides in assisting operators to make the best decision. A number of them have also eased the pressure on control room staff by greater use of direct lines and setting up help desks to deal with callers who are simply seeking advice or information. Central Scotland used financial sponsorship from Mercury Communications to publicise its Crime Management Unit. After just six months of operation, well over 50 per cent of crimes are now reported directly to the Unit, and the figure is expected to continue rising.

86. Another relevant initiative is Oxford's Customer Services Department, which incorporates the Area's crime desk, public information service, and a resource management function to relieve patrol officers of some incident attendance. Set up in 1995 as a pilot project, it is already handling around 500 calls per day from the public. Kent has also taken the help desk approach further with its Resource Desk. Officers staffing the Desk offer advice and information as well as resolving many incidents that would formerly have required officer deployment, using a combination of telephone enquiries and directed officer attendance (Case Study 1). These examples illustrate the importance of effective handling of telephone demand (Exhibit 21, overleaf). The public is more likely to accept non-attendance by police officers to certain types of incident when forces answer calls promptly and resolve matters satisfactorily over the telephone. A measure of success for the future may be greater *accessibility*, rather than simply visibility.

Case Study 1
Kent's Resource Desk

Kent Constabulary recently tried out the use of a Resource Desk to handle, and where possible resolve, a number of calls without deploying patrol officers. The Desk was staffed for the purposes of the trial by two inspectors, to whom the control room referred all non-urgent calls for assessment of the appropriate response. This initial short trial was designed to test the principle of 'alternative resourcing':

- the trial indicated that a Resource Desk had the potential to reduce incident attendance by 40 per cent, thereby freeing up significant patrol officer time for more proactive work;

- the Desk resolved many difficult incidents, such as reports of nuisance, where the conventional approach of attendance by a patrol officer is often seen to be unsatisfactory to the public. The trial demonstrated that, over time, the Desk was able to encourage the development of long-term solutions to reported problems, with other agencies and individuals playing their part;

- caller satisfaction was very high. A follow-up survey of 38 respondents indicated that all were satisfied with the way their call had been handled;

- the location of the Desk away from the control room was important in devising innovative approaches to resolving incidents;

- the facility ideally needs to be staffed by experienced constables; and

- the trial provided sufficiently positive data to prompt the force to conduct a six-month operational evaluation.

One illustration of the Resource Desk approach concerned a complaint about youths who were causing a nuisance by riding motorbikes across wasteland opposite a terrace of houses. The first action was to find out who owned the land; on discovering that it belonged to a nearby army base, the officer telephoned the base to inform them of the problem. Army personnel were promptly dispatched and they not only dispersed the youths but made sure they could not return by securing the perimeter fence. This was clearly a cost-effective police response – it also presented an opportunity for a police officer to visit the householders and inform them of a successful outcome, thus enhancing positive contacts with the community.

Source: Kent County Constabulary

Streetwise
Effective Police Patrol

Exhibit 21
Making graded response work

Effective handling of calls by
the control room can make
graded response work better.

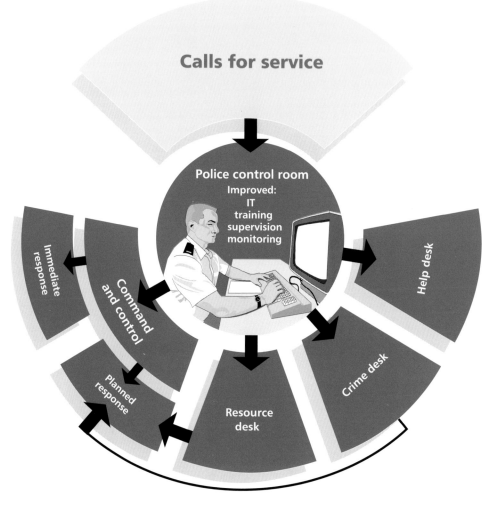

Calls for service

Police control room
Improved:
IT
training
supervision
monitoring

Help desk

Immediate
response

Command
and control

Crime desk

Planned
response

Resource
desk

*Note: It may be appropriate,
especially in smaller forces/control
rooms, to integrate the crime desk,
help desk and resource desk; Thames
Valley is piloting this approach in its
Oxford BCU.*

Source: Audit Commission

Matching resources to demand

87. Making graded response work is essential, but better management of demand does not stop at the initial response stage. Improvements are also possible in matching operational resources to patterns of demand from the public, and in making better use of the contributions from non-police sources. This would help forces absorb the rise in reactive workload without sacrificing proactivity and reassurance patrol. Specifically, forces should consider how to build on recent initiatives to:

♦ develop optimal shift patterns;

♦ improve the management of abstractions from patrol duties;

♦ tap the potential of other contributions to community safety and patrol, specifically Special Constables and CCTV;

♦ draw on good practice in partnership working.

Shift patterns and abstractions

88. Forces need shift systems that bring the right number of officers on duty at the right time, so as to provide both minimum cover and flexible deployment. This may require amendment of national regulations governing shift working to allow more local customising of shift patterns. Cambridgeshire has experimented successfully with a flexible three-shift system – the day shift operates between 6am and 4pm and the night shift from 4pm until 6am (with the third shift on rest days). Starting times vary according to local demand patterns and the working day for each officer lasts from eight to ten hours. A better match might also be obtained by greater use of part-time police officers – there are currently only around 1,000 out of a total strength of 127,000.

89. A high level of abstraction is a principal reason why foot patrol is limited in many areas. Where information systems permit, forces should monitor abstraction levels across the force and set internal benchmarks to keep the issue on managers' agendas. Particular attention should be paid to sickness absence, the main unplanned cause of abstraction. If forces took appropriate management action to try to reduce average absence levels per officer from 12 days each year to 10 days, this would generate the equivalent of almost 1,000 additional police officers. The fact that the average annual sickness level is currently below 10 days per officer in about one-fifth of forces suggests that this is a realistic target.

Getting the best from additional contributions to patrol effort

90. The dearth of police officers undertaking targeted, high visibility patrol has inevitably led to searches for other solutions, both public sector and private. In acknowledging that the police cannot do it all, local authorities and police authorities may increasingly need to adopt the role of informed purchasers of community safety provision, from a spectrum of possibilities that extends well beyond regular police officers (Exhibit 22, overleaf). Principal among these are Special Constables, traffic wardens, CCTV and private security guards.

Streetwise
Effective Police Patrol

Exhibit 22
The community safety spectrum

The police are the most important, but not the only, contributor to community safety.

	Powers	Coverage	Accountable to	Training	Unit cost per year (including overheads)
Volunteers	Citizens' powers	Public areas	No one	None	Negligible
Private security guards	Citizens' powers	Stipulated in contract	Employer	3 days if BS7499 applies	£12,000
Resident & mobile caretakers	Citizens' powers	Local authority estates	Employer	Limited to caretaking role	£18,000
Local authority patrol officers	Citizens' powers	Public and private areas controlled by local authority	Local authority	4 weeks leading to NVQ (Security)	£18,000
Parks police	Limited to by-law enforcement	Open spaces under the control of the local authority	Local authority	6 weeks initial training	£21,000
CCTV	N/A	Limited areas of (mostly) town centres	Dependent upon monitoring arrangements	Limited training for monitoring staff	Set up cost £250,000; ongoing revenue cost varies, typically £140,000 a year
Traffic wardens	Regulation of traffic and parking	Force area	Chief constable	2 weeks induction/traffic regulations	£22,000
Special Constables	Full police powers – eg, arrest, stop and search, legitimate use of force	Force and neighbouring force areas	Chief constable	10 weekends initial plus ad hoc training	Variable, but best estimate is £1,500
Auxiliary patrol officers	Restricted police powers	Force area	Chief constable	Similar to parks police?	£25,000 (estimate)
Regular police officers	Full police powers – eg, arrest, stop and search, legitimate use of force	England and Wales	Chief constable	15 weeks block training plus tutoring and in-force training over 2 years	£32,000

Source: Audit Commission

91. There are numerous examples of innovation in the use of Specials, such as the Northamptonshire approach of training them to execute warrants and assist in post-arrest searches. Hertfordshire deploys some Specials on core shift patterns to work with regular officers, and has assigned them particular responsibility for mounting anti-vandalism patrols near schools. Milton Keynes Area is compiling a skills profile to ensure that it makes the most of Specials' expertise.

92. Assuming that forces do resolve the problems around training and deployment, there is a limit to how far they can rely on the contribution of Specials, given their purely voluntary status. Paying a retainer to those able to guarantee, say, eight to sixteen hours a week could be a cost-effective way of increasing the contribution of Special Constables, and thus boosting the presence on the streets of skilled patrol officers accountable to the chief constable. This would bring Specials more in line with the remuneration of retained firefighters, although the actual level of payment, and the implications for employer-liability insurance, would need consideration. The income from charging for persistent false alarms might be used to pump-prime such an initiative.[1] Clearly, forces would want to apply selection criteria to those Specials applying for a retainer, and those who could not commit more than a few hours a week, or who were otherwise deemed ineligible for payment, might continue to contribute their services on the current unpaid basis. In considering the pros and cons of this proposal, lessons can be learnt from previous experiments in making 'bounty' payments to Specials (Exhibit 23 and Appendix 4).

[1]
As an illustration, income of around £9 million from charges for call-outs to false alarms could pay for the enhanced or guaranteed hours of around 3,000 Specials if retainers were set at £3,000 per year. Income from false alarms would probably decline over time.

Exhibit 23
Paying a retainer to Special Constables

Consideration needs to be given to the pros and cons of paying Special Constables.

Source: Audit Commission

Advantages	Disadvantages
Specials would have more incentive to increase, or at least guarantee, the hours they currently commit; this would enable forces to plan their use more effectively.	Payment might undermine the voluntary ethos and commitment of those who are currently willing to work without payment.
Specials would be more accountable for the work they perform.	Payment might attract the 'wrong type' of recruit, doing it only for the money.
Recruitment and retention could be less problematic, especially in urban areas.	The funds needed to pay the retainer would take resources away from regular policing and may antagonise police officers.
Forces would have more incentive to ensure that Specials were managed well.	A retainer scheme may be expensive and/or cumbersome to administer.
The status of Specials could be enhanced; payment would be a tangible sign of the value that forces attach to Specials.	

Exhibit 24
Levels of public reassurance

Police officers (on foot and in cars) and CCTV reassure the public, but traffic wardens do not.

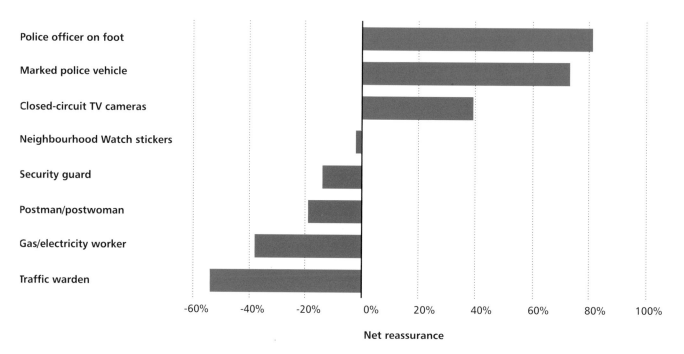

Note: 'Net reassurance' is the percentage of respondents who said they were very/fairly reassured by the sight of, say, CCTV minus the percentage who were not very/not at all reassured by CCTV.

Source: MORI survey conducted on behalf of the Audit Commission

93. Another uniformed presence on the streets that could be better used is the corps of traffic wardens; currently numbering 5,000, this figure is likely to be reduced as more local authorities gradually take on the parking enforcement role. Although wardens possess limited powers, they are trained and managed by police officers, are linked to police stations by radio and work predominantly in town centres or residential areas. They are thus a potentially high-profile, visible presence and it is in forces' interest to project a greater reassurance profile for traffic wardens (Exhibit 24). This could be achieved through improved management[1] and active promotion of the essential role which wardens perform.

[1]
See the Audit Commission's
report, *Fine Lines: Improving
the Traffic Warden Service*,
HMSO, 1992.

'...CCTV has been important in reclaiming public spaces...'

Candid cameras: the role of CCTV

94. CCTV cameras are an increasingly common sight in town centres. Early evaluation suggests that CCTV has been important in reclaiming public spaces and revitalising many areas which were in danger of becoming ghost towns in the evenings. The impact on levels of the types of crime that are committed mostly in public, such as car theft and street disorder, is often significant, especially in the early days of a scheme. In King's Lynn, for example, thefts of and from cars fell by more than 90 per cent in the first year that the town centre was covered by CCTV, and the figures remain consistently low. Publicising these successes obviously has an impact on public reassurance, which can be enhanced by advertising the presence of the cameras. Many cameras are placed above the line of sight and invisible cameras do not reassure or deter as effectively as those in clear view. A further benefit of CCTV has emerged from the scheme in Newcastle upon Tyne; there has been a significant increase in guilty pleas when offenders have been confronted with visual evidence, thus saving valuable police time in court.

95. The success of many existing schemes has led to a clamour for more and more CCTV, though there are risks in seeking quick technological fixes for complex problems. At around £250,000 per scheme, plus annual running costs of possibly £150,000, it can represent a sound investment – a round-the-clock presence by a patrol officer would cost in the region of £200,000 – but CCTV only supplements police patrol and is not a substitute for it. Local authorities, police forces and business groups should carry out joint evaluations to answer such questions as:

- what problems will CCTV address? Is CCTV the best solution?

- how will the risk of displacing criminal activity to other areas be countered?

- what are the criteria for the scheme's success; how will these be measured?

- what technical specification will best deliver the scheme's objectives?

- who will monitor the system: the police or other agencies?

- will monitoring be on a 24-hours a day basis, or more limited (and thus cheaper)?

- who will pay the ongoing revenue costs?

Of pressing importance is the need to incorporate into every CCTV scheme robust safeguards against abuse of the system, such as unauthorised access to tapes. A nationwide code of practice, preferably with statutory back up, should be formulated and agreed as soon as is practicable.

Streetwise
Effective Police Patrol

Exhibit 25
Advantages and disadvantages of auxiliary patrol officers

There would be financial benefits, but practical difficulties, in having auxiliary patrol officers.

Advantages	Disadvantages
Enhanced visible presence, so increasing public reassurance.	Appointment of auxiliaries within existing budgets would reduce the number of regular officers; if significant, this could constrain operational flexibility.
Potential to increase overall staffing levels within existing budget.	
Staff are recruited for patrol work only, increasing scope for stable assignments and greater identification with the locality.	Public may lose confidence in the police if auxiliaries are seen as 'second class' PCs.
Keeps auxiliary patrol work within police control and full public accountability.	Auxiliary officers may face situations which they are not trained to deal with; this may impose more rather than less pressure on regular officers.
High-profile patrol work carried out by staff employed and trained just for that role, rather than on sufferance.	

Sources: Report of the ACPO Patrol Project Working Group, May 1995 and Audit Commission analysis

Auxiliary patrol officers

96. There was some debate during 1995 on the feasibility of auxiliary or 'designated' patrol officers, mooted in a discussion paper issued by the Cassels Inquiry[1] and subsequently rejected by ACPO as unworkable. Such officers would be paid less than constables but would be part of the local constabulary and authorised, after appropriate training, to exercise limited street powers such as arrests for minor public order offences and simple thefts. Although it would offer financial benefits, this option poses practical difficulties (Exhibit 25). Some forces have found it difficult to integrate non-police staff, such as civilians and traffic wardens, with police officers. A repetition of this difficulty would prevent the benefits of auxiliary patrol officers from being realised. There is also a likelihood that creating a less well-paid auxiliary tier would diminish the status of patrol even further. Improvements in the organisation and impact of current patrol work may diminish further interest in auxiliary patrol, unless these improvements fail to increase public satisfaction with patrol levels.

[1] Independent Committee of Inquiry into the Roles and Responsibilities of the Police, established by the Police Foundation and the Policy Studies Institute under the chairmanship of Sir John Cassels.

Targeting patrol work

97. Current efforts to manage demand more efficiently and make appropriate use of Special Constables are essential to create time for proactivity, but managers must then ensure that this time is used effectively. All forces should follow the good practice applied by some in:

◆ setting clear objectives for patrol and monitoring their achievement;

◆ encouraging a problem-solving approach at local level, especially through assigning officers to geographical areas; and

◆ improving briefings and tasking.

Setting clear objectives

98. There are lessons to be learnt from a rich vein of experience in setting objectives for policing. Success is most likely to be achieved when objectives:

◆ are tightly defined rather than abstract and unfocused;

◆ are set in the context of the area's crime and incident patterns;

◆ specify the location and times when problems occur;

◆ define the scale of the problem;

◆ avoid legal or control room jargon in describing the problem or task;

◆ specify what impact the targeted action is intended to have; and

◆ are monitored regularly by sergeants to determine whether revision is needed.

99. The particular methods used to identify problems and define tasks will vary according to local circumstances and the quality of IT support. Surrey Police uses team briefings every two weeks to agree the tasks that will be assigned to officers when they are not dealing with an incident. The list is passed to the control room and the operators work down it to deploy officers accordingly. Although other forces use a similar team-based approach, Surrey's use of control room prompts increases the chance that officers' activities will match the prioritised tasks.

100. More detailed tasking helps ensure greater visibility, using analysis to determine *where* and *when* reassurance is most needed and clarifying *how* patrol officers' presence can have the most impact. This is the essence of reassurance patrol. The Commission's survey of the public showed that people in inner cities give a very high priority to patrols on large housing estates and outside schools at the end of the afternoon. In quieter areas such as small towns and villages, police presence at pubs and clubs at closing time is given a similarly high priority. Recent research suggests that patrol effort aimed specifically at reassuring people in vulnerable areas needs to target disorderly behaviour – a prime source of anxiety – and maximise police officers' contact with citizens.[1]

[1] Professor Michael Hough, *Anxiety about Crime: Findings from the 1994 British Crime Survey,* Home Office Research Study No. 147, 1995.

Streetwise
Effective Police Patrol

Exhibit 26
Officers' contacts with the public

Surveys completed by patrol officers at the end of their shifts can provide insights into their contacts with the public.

Nature of contact initiated by officer

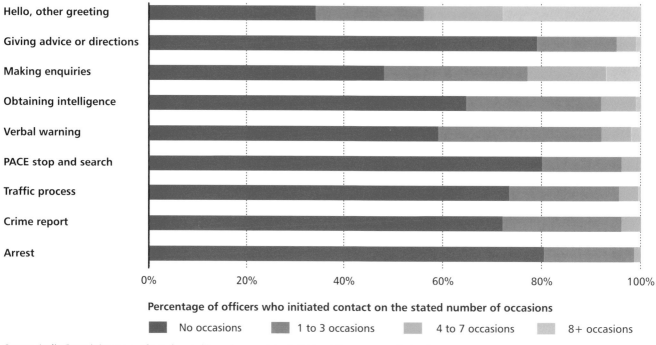

Percentage of officers who initiated contact on the stated number of occasions

No occasions   1 to 3 occasions   4 to 7 occasions   8+ occasions

Source: Audit Commission survey of patrol constables and sergeants in six fieldwork forces on a particular day

Using performance indicators to target patrol work and monitor achievement

101. There is little point in setting targets for patrol work if managers do not then monitor their achievement. As with some other aspects of policing, it is not easy to reach a consensus about which performance indicators (PIs) best measure the success of directed patrol in achieving policy objectives. There is particular interest in assessing a vital feature of patrol work – contact with the public. This has been difficult to capture in terms of quality, and not just quantity, of interactions. Activity sampling has provided some insights into how officers use their time, but it can usefully be supplemented by surveys designed to gauge levels and types of citizen contact (Exhibit 26). It is important not to overstate the precision of such surveys, but forces need to start somewhere in trying to quantify these contacts. Supervisors should consider whether these results hold any surprises or lessons – what actions do they prompt? They may, for example, reflect a need for guidelines setting out what is expected from patrolling officers, especially on how, when and where to engage with the public.

102. PIs thus have a role to play, but because patrol work is community-based in nature, care is needed in setting any national performance measures. However, extensive discussions with practitioners show that a set of measures can be devised (Exhibit 27). Police managers can choose from this menu according to local circumstances. Some measures are used already, others may be collectable only if IT or other systems permit – for example, PIs on calls to repeat locations. Whichever indicators are used, they should always be set alongside qualitative assessments by supervisors of individual patrol officers' work.

Exhibit 27
Performance indicators for patrol work

Monitoring achievement requires clear objectives and the selection of appropriate indicators for each objective.

Enhance resources for operational patrol	Provide reassurance through high visibility patrol	Respond appropriately to incidents	Maintain public order and deal effectively with problems of anti-social behaviour	Make effective use of intelligence to support force and local objectives, notably to tackle crime effectively
Uniformed PCs as percentage of strength	Percentage of uniformed PCs' time spent in public	Percentage of incidents graded 'immediate response'	Percentage change in public order incidents	Number of intelligence submissions per officer: – percentage leading to arrest or other positive action
Percentage of uniformed PCs designated as patrol	Percentage of uniformed PCs' time on preventive patrol	Percentage of incidents allocated a delayed response	Percentage of disorder calls which are to repeat locations	Percentage of crime reports submitted within deadlines
Abstraction levels on reliefs	Identification of key locations/times for patrol: – achievement of targets for patrol in key spots	Percentage of incidents attended by patrol officers	Officers' satisfaction with inter-agency efforts	Percentage of PNC checks resulting in action
Days lost through sickness per patrol officer		Officers' satisfaction with control room decisions	Officer days lost through assault	Arrests and traffic process cases per officer
Specials as a percentage of regular officer strength	Quantified contacts with citizens	Achievement of target response times		Number of stop and search checks per officer: – percentage on known offenders – percentage leading to arrest or other action
Average hours per week worked by Specials	Public surveys: seen police patrol in last 2 days	Victim/caller satisfaction with response (survey)		
	Public surveys: satisfaction with level of patrol			Percentage of beats for which up-to-date profiles (key information and analysis) exist

Source: Audit Commission

Box C
**Local solutions to local problems:
racial attacks on an inner-city estate**

Sources: National Audit Office and Metropolitan Police Service

A local beat officer discussed with community leaders the growing problem of racial attacks and harassment in an inner-city area. Such incidents had doubled between 1993 and 1994, but in many cases witnesses felt too intimidated to assist the police and local authority in challenging the attackers. On the basis of the beat officer's research and gathering of local intelligence, a number of suspects and vulnerable locations were identified; a sophisticated proactive operation was mounted involving decoy officers and surveillance work. As a result of the first operation, four suspects were arrested and later convicted of offences under the Public Order Act; a second operation was equally successful in terms of arrests and prosecutions. Officers are not complacent that the problem has been eradicated, but the number of racial attacks has decreased since the operation and a degree of reassurance has been provided to local ethnic minority communities.

Encouraging a problem-solving approach

103. More than any other core police activity, patrol work is based around small and often discrete geographical areas. It therefore lends itself to tailor-made solutions to local problems, from meeting the reassurance needs of vulnerable people to tackling lower-level crime and disorder. Problem-solving already occurs widely on an ad hoc basis (Box C) and in good practice areas officers systematically adopt this approach. This requires computerised information systems, an analytical capacity and training in the necessary skills – especially for sergeants and inspectors, who are best placed to analyse problems across the area and devise solutions. Because few forces have all the elements in place, the transition from reactive policing is likely to be a gradual process, but tangible benefits will become evident.

Geographic policing

104. A cultural, as opposed to technical, requirement is that individual officers take ownership of problems. Some forces have sought to push ownership of policing problems down the chain of command and improve local awareness through geographic or sector policing (Case Study 2). The theory behind geographic policing is that if all the basic policing needs of a relatively small area are allocated to a particular group of officers, they will be more likely to seek solutions to the long-term problems which underlie many calls for service in their area. The officers know that the problems of today will be their problems tomorrow and the day after, and so on until they are resolved. While clearly an advance on no ownership at all, team ownership requires good leadership if it is to have as much impact as when individual officers assume a personal responsibility to get to the bottom of a difficulty.

Case Study 2
Sector policing in the Metropolitan Police Service (MPS)

The MPS introduced sector policing from 1990 onwards to focus police activity on community needs and encourage officers to take more ownership of local problems. Instead of dividing resources across a block of time, Divisions are split into a number of geographic 'sectors' for which officers have 24-hour responsibility. Each Division is allowed some flexibility in applying general principles to particular circumstances. West Hendon covers 14 square miles and has 183 uniformed constables on strength; it is divided into three sectors, each with an inspector in overall charge and six sergeant-led teams. Three teams fulfil core responsibilities – incident response, patrol and station duties – around the clock, while the other three are either on rest days, supporting core policing at peak periods or undertaking proactive work.

Flexible shift patterns have ensured that there is a good match between demand and deployment; the MPS's Charter targets for response times are met and the evidence available from public forums is that local people are reasonably satisfied with visibility levels. There are difficulties to work through – some are practical ones such as a shortage of radios at peak deployment times. There are also cultural issues such as a degree of parochialism – sector teams were reluctant, for example, to release officers for football duties that fell outside the Division, and this is now controlled centrally. Sector policing across the MPS is monitored constantly to ensure that appropriate steps are taken to overcome the difficulties.

Demand and deployment data, averaged for all Wednesdays, February to April 1995

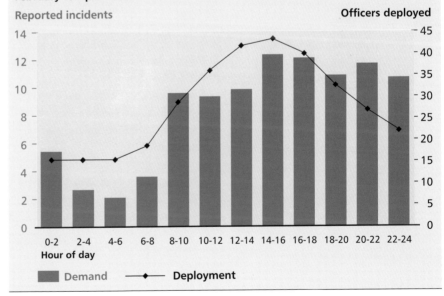

Sources: National Audit Office and the MPS

105. Another rationale for geographic policing is that it promotes continuity in personal contacts with members of the public – not only do officers get to know their area, they also become better known by local people. This leads to better flows of information and greater sensitivity to local needs. The Commission's public survey offers some support for the existence of a link between satisfaction and the degree to which people can identify with a local 'bobby' (Exhibit 28, overleaf).

106. There are many variations in the way that geographic policing is implemented. For example, some forces have opted not for sector policing but

Exhibit 28
What influences public satisfaction?

There is no link between visibility and public satisfaction, but satisfaction is higher where people know their local 'bobby'.

Source: Audit Commission analysis of MORI public survey data in five force areas

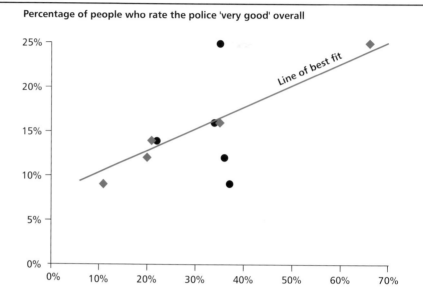

Percentage of people who rate the police 'very good' overall

Line of best fit

Percentage of people in an area who:

● saw a police officer in the previous week

◆ knew or recognised a police officer

for a hybrid approach, whereby separate teams of officers carry out rapid-response work and community-based patrol. There is no blueprint that will suit every circumstance. Whichever route forces pursue to get closer to the communities they serve, they need to inculcate a more proactive, learning approach in every officer, even those whose principal role is incident response. Where officers have been given territorial responsibilities, their appraisal should cover the identification of policing problems and the proposal of workable solutions.

Improving briefings and tasking

107. Daily briefings should link high-level strategy with the tactics of day-to-day operational work. Briefings will have greater impact if they are short, well prepared, relevant to immediate local problems and, wherever possible, exploit new technology such as videos and geographic mapping systems. Good briefings and debriefings help to promote a learning culture, where information and experiences are shared in order to achieve continuous improvement in performance. While informal contacts between sergeants and constables can help achieve this, officers attach a high value to learning from each other and therefore opportunities to bring the team together at the end of the shift should be explored. Involving local intelligence officers and crime pattern analysts in these discussions is a way of tapping expertise and sharing ideas across shifts. Where it is simply not practicable to debrief at the end of the shift, team leaders should identify other opportunities such as the overlap period on a variable shift system. Debriefing also has a welfare benefit, allowing officers who have experienced a difficult or stressful situation to talk it through with their supervisor and colleagues.

Case Study 3
Enhancing the status of patrol: beat managers

Killingbeck in Leeds is a busy, inner-city division; its 190 uniformed constables dealt with more than 70,000 incidents and 25,000 reported crimes in 1994 – 48 per cent and 82 per cent respectively above the national average. It has 17 foot beats, each covered by a beat manager; these officers are grouped in six teams, managed by two sergeants. Each officer has drawn up a beat profile identifying the characteristics of the area and spelling out the local problems, mainly of crime and nuisance. This is accompanied by an Action Plan, often formulated jointly with other agencies such as the local housing department, and discussed regularly with the sergeant. The Plan sets out the beat manager's long, medium and short-term objectives and focuses on the underlying causes of problems which result in repeat calls to the police. These are often extremely specific – for example, an alleyway between two empty council houses was being used to gain access to waste ground where stolen cars were being dumped. The solutions are not always ones of police enforcement – in this case, the officer asked the council to block the alleyway with a skip.

The beat managers need to be close to the community to be effective problem-solvers (several live in the area they police) and make a commitment to serve in the post for three to five years. After initially having to challenge perceptions of being old-style community constables, the posts are now recognised as interesting, challenging and a stepping-stone for ambitious officers.

Source : West Yorkshire Police

Raising the status of patrol and enhancing supervision

108. Police managers should ensure that time carved out for proactivity is used effectively – in the short-term, improvements in direction and targeting of patrol activities should help. But to ensure long-term success, they must also address the relatively low status of patrol work, especially walking a beat. Changing the perception that beat work is the bottom rung of the ladder is difficult and will take time because it requires changes in both working practices and, perhaps more importantly, cultural views about what constitutes real police work. The Sheehy Inquiry[1] argued for a greater focus on front-line officers working round-the-clock shifts, and recommended a financial premium to reflect the importance of patrol duties. The Inquiry's view gained support in some quarters but was not accepted by the Home Secretary. There are, however, other ways of tackling the status issue and making beat work more rewarding.

109. Some are linked to lateral career development, such as accrediting beat-manager status to more posts and assigning them key responsibilities such as multi-agency partnership work (Case Study 3, above and 4, overleaf). Senior officers need to back their assertions that patrol is the most important job in policing with action to improve uniforms, equipment and the working environment, and to try to limit the depletion of patrol sections to fill gaps elsewhere by stricter adherence to target levels of staffing. The service may also wish to review the practice of basing probationers in patrol sections for almost the whole of their two years. Instead of beat work being seen as simply laying the foundations for specialist police work, why not use specialist assignments to develop probationers and then assess them individually to see whether they are equipped to take on the demanding role of beat manager?

[1]
Inquiry into Police Responsibilities and Rewards, set up by the Government and chaired by Sir Patrick Sheehy; it reported in June 1993.

Case Study 4
Enhancing the status of patrol:
ward-based policing

The city of Plymouth has in recent years experienced economic decline with the shrinking of the naval establishment – unemployment levels on some large estates exceed 40 per cent. The policing problems in the city are severe, and some areas suffer from unusually high rates of violent and anti-social behaviour. In 1994 the force revised its approach to policing the city. The traditional mix of core shifts and (increasingly isolated) community constables was replaced by two main groupings of response teams and ward-based officers. Around 150 officers, split into five sections with 30 officers each, provide fast response around the clock, while some 120 officers working in 13 teams carry out the remaining patrol tasks.

The teams' areas correspond to the city's 13 electoral wards, and the officers are expected to work almost exclusively on foot. Their core duties are to foster community links, undertake proactive crime work, follow up incidents handled initially by the fast-response officers, and liaise with other agencies with a role in the ward. Regular meetings are held which bring together the police, elected representatives, statutory and voluntary agencies and members of the community in each ward. The split between reactive and proactive work is reinforced by the fact that the two groups operate on different radio channels. This scheme has been running for just over a year and has not yet been subject to formal evaluation; the expectation is that the approach will increase public reassurance, reduce crime levels, increase detections, raise the status of the patrol constable and strengthen inter-agency links.

Source: Devon and Cornwall Constabulary

Leadership on the streets: supervision and tutoring

110. Inspectors carry heavy workloads and the reduction in the number of senior officers has increased the managerial element of their role. For sergeants, too, there are plenty of jobs to do that keep them in the station, including checking the products of constables' work such as crime reports. However, constables will perform well those tasks that are valued, and an effective way for managers to impart a sense of importance to patrol work is to do it themselves on an appropriate number of occasions. Their expertise should allow them to add value and, more importantly, set leadership examples out on the streets.

111. The paperwork burden could be reduced through wider use of accreditation – formal recognition that an officer is capable of performing particular tasks to a defined standard, and thus requires minimal supervision in carrying out those tasks. For example, Surrey accredits constables who achieve an agreed standard for file submission, thus relieving sergeants of the need to check those files frequently. Time freed up for sergeants can then be used to identify policing problems, agree how these will be tackled, assess the quality of their officers' work and provide them with feedback. It is essential that, in the drive to get more constables on patrol, the need for sufficient sergeants to supervise their work is not overlooked.

112. Tutoring is an important technique in preparing probationers for beat work, but selection and evaluation of tutors could be improved. Dedicated probationer units, as developed by North Wales Police and others, should be encouraged. It may also be useful to offer guidelines on a minimum level of *tutored* foot patrol to be undertaken by probationers. The work of tutors should be quality assured; officers may require refresher training in areas such as new legislation if they have been tutors for many years. The curriculum for the training of probationers is currently being reviewed to ensure that it covers skills appropriate to the changing nature of patrol work; fieldwork for this study points to work with young people, beat management and problem-solving as areas that merit more attention.

113. It is a tribute to the commitment and professionalism of police patrol officers that their role continues to be so highly valued by the public. Despite the pressure on resources posed by other demands such as responding promptly to emergencies, patrol on foot and in cars is still integral to the style of policing in this country, and is vital in fostering good community relations. Directed, intelligence-driven patrol has a key role to play in the model of policing described in this report, but it is only one element of a policing strategy and not a complete strategy in itself. If the police service responds as positively to the recommendations in this report as it did to the Commission's report on the investigation of crime, public reassurance could be strengthened and the quality of life improved.

'...patrol on foot and in cars is still integral to the style of policing in this country...'

Recommendations

To the Home Office and police authorities:

1 Publicise when it is appropriate to call out the police and use the 999 system

2 Consider the costs and benefits of a public information helpline, possibly using a 333 number

3 Acknowledge that foot patrol is not a panacea for all policing problems

4 Improve communication channels between police and the public; strive for consensus about policing priorities and ways of tackling nuisance and anti-social behaviour

5 Consider putting community safety partnerships on a statutory footing

6 Amend national regulations to permit more local flexibility in shift systems

7 Agree a method for evaluating CCTV and safeguarding against abuse

8 Consider giving forces greater flexibility to pay retainers to Special Constables

To the public:

9 Recognise that some calls for police service can best be dealt with by telephone

10 Be aware of criteria for using the 999 system

11 Acknowledge the value but also limitations of foot patrol

To police forces:

12 Improve the application of graded response by
- assessing emergencies more accurately
- screening incidents that do not require police attendance

13 Monitor the implementation of graded response

14 Improve training and supervision of control room staff

15 Consider help desks to deal with some calls from the public

16 Analyse calls for service to identify repeat locations

17 Review shift patterns; improve management of abstractions, especially sickness

18 Make better use of Special Constables

19 Set objectives for patrol; develop quantitative and qualitative performance indicators to track performance

20 Set targets for high visibility patrol and monitor achievement

21 Task officers so that non-incident time is applied to local objectives

22 Encourage the adoption of a problem-solving approach by all officers

23 Assign geographic responsibilities to more officers

24 Improve briefings and expand use of debriefings

25 Strive to enhance the status of beat patrol

26 Improve tutoring and supervise the process of patrol on the streets

Appendix 1: Forces visited during the study

Main fieldwork forces

- Dyfed-Powys Police
- Greater Manchester Police
- Lancashire Constabulary
- Nottinghamshire Constabulary
- Surrey Police
- Metropolitan Police Service (fieldwork by the National Audit Office)

Other forces studied

- Central Scotland Police
- Cleveland Constabulary
- Devon and Cornwall Constabulary
- Kent County Constabulary
- Northamptonshire Police
- Northumbria Police
- Royal Ulster Constabulary
- Sussex Police
- Thames Valley Police
- West Yorkshire Police

Appendix 2: Members of Advisory Panel and Working Group

Members of the ACPO Advisory Panel

- Mr David Blakey, Chief Constable, West Mercia Constabulary
- Mr David Burke, Chief Constable, North Yorkshire Police
- Mr Keith Povey, Chief Constable, Leicestershire Constabulary
- Mr Ray White, Chief Constable, Dyfed-Powys Police

Members of the Advisory Panel were nominated by ACPO.

Members of the Study Working Group

- Chief Inspector Steve Allen, Avon and Somerset Constabulary
- Superintendent Matt Baggott, Metropolitan Police Service
- Superintendent Roy Bailey, Thames Valley Police
- John Burrows, Morgan, Harris, Burrows Consultants
- Chief Inspector John Donnison, Leicestershire Constabulary
- Inspector Alan Evans, Northumbria Police
- Inspector Carl Puiy, Suffolk Constabulary
- Chief Inspector Keith Rogers, Surrey Police
- Chief Inspector Phil Rogerson, South Yorkshire Police
- Inspector Mark Sheasby, West Midlands Police

Members of the Working Group contributed in a personal capacity.

Other acknowledgements

Additional comments on draft reports were provided by Mr Bob Hunt, formerly Assistant Commissioner in the Metropolitan Police; Professor Mike Hough from South Bank University; and Miss Margaret Clayton, formerly Assistant Under-Secretary of State in the Home Office Police Department.

The public survey research commissioned from MORI was managed by Simon Braunholtz, with the support of Warren Hatter and Sally Taylor.

The Commission gratefully acknowledges the contribution of these individuals and those in the fieldwork forces, but recognises that responsibility for the contents of the report rests with it alone.

Appendix 3: Surveys and questionnaires

Survey of public attitudes to police patrol

A survey of residents in five geographical areas was conducted by MORI on behalf of the Audit Commission; quantitative findings are based on the analysis of 801 home interviews, supplemented by a qualitative phase based on six focus groups.

Quantitative survey

Five survey areas were selected by the Audit Commission, drawn from the sites of fieldwork undertaken in police operational units. The five areas were Camberley (Surrey), Haverfordwest (Dyfed-Powys), Arnold (Nottinghamshire), Leyland (Lancashire) and Moss Side/Withington (Greater Manchester).

A total of 22 questions were covered in the interviews, grouped around five issues: visibility and frequency of patrols in the area; the effect of patrols, especially in terms of reassurance; willingness to pay for increased patrols; views on specific aspects of police performance; and priorities for improving community safety.

In each of the five areas a representative quota of around 160 adults were interviewed in their homes during June 1995. The samples were constructed by identifying all enumeration districts (EDs) in the area, listed by ward, from which a random sample of EDs was selected. In each selected ED, interviewers were set quotas of respondents by sex, age (18-24, 25-34, 35-54 and 55+), employment status (working full-time, not working full-time) and ethnicity.

In addition, 129 booster interviews were conducted in the vicinity of police stations in four residential areas. The purpose was to examine possible differences in perception between this group and the population as a whole; data from the booster survey has not been combined with the main sample data. The data in both main and booster samples is unweighted.

It is possible to predict the variation between the sample results and the 'true' values that would have been obtained had the total population been interviewed, at the 95 per cent confidence level – ie, the chances are 95 in 100 that the 'true' value will fall within the specified range. The predicted ranges for a sample size of 800 and percentage results at the 95 per cent confidence level are as follows:

Approximate sampling tolerances applicable to percentages at or near these levels:

10% or 90%	30% or 70%	50%
+/- 3%	+/- 5%	+/- 6%

Thus if 30% of the sample gave a particular answer, the chances are 95 in 100 that the 'true' value will fall within 5 percentage points of the sample result.

Qualitative survey

Before the sample survey, MORI conducted a qualitative study consisting of six focus group discussions, facilitated by an experienced member of the MORI team. These group discussions informed the design of the questionnaire, as well as giving depth to understanding people's views on the impact of police patrols.

The groups were as follows:

Group 1 – Manchester (Moss Side): women, aged 18-30, social groups C1, C2, D, E and including quota for ethnic minorities

Group 2 – Manchester (Withington): mixed sex, aged 31-60, B, C1, C2 and including quota for ethnic minorities

Group 3 – Haverfordwest: mixed sex, aged 18-40, B, C1, C2 and D

Group 4 – Havefordwest: mixed sex, aged 31-60, B, C1, C2, and D

Group 5 – Camberley: mixed sex, aged over 50, B, C1 and C2

Group 6 – Camberley: mixed sex, aged 18-40, social class AB

Questionnaire to sample of basic command units

Most forces are structured around command units based on a geographical area, delivering the bulk of policing services with specialist support from HQ. They are usually commanded by an officer of superintendent rank. Although they may be called areas, divisions or districts, the generic term 'basic command unit' (BCU) is widely recognised.

A questionnaire covering a range of patrol-related issues was sent to a sample of BCUs drawn from each of the 41 provincial forces in England and Wales. Two BCUs were selected in small forces, three in medium-sized forces and four from large forces. Some 112 completed returns from BCUs have been analysed.

Survey of patrol constables and sergeants

To supplement the structured interviews and other elements of fieldwork, a sample of patrol constables and sergeants in the six fieldwork forces was asked to complete a questionnaire. This covered patrol activities and officers' views on topics such as control room decisions, awareness of objectives and the value of patrol work.

Questionnaires were sent to the 12 BCUs where fieldwork was undertaken, with a request that all constables and sergeants on duty on a particular day in June 1995 be given a copy to complete. The completed questionnaires were returned directly to the Audit Commission. A total of 409 questionnaires were received from constables and 81 from sergeants. The response rate can only be estimated because the study team was aware only of how many questionnaires were sent to BCUs (the number being based on the establishment of patrol constables and sergeants), not how many were distributed on the day. The estimated response rate of 33 per cent is likely to be an under-estimate, taking into account abstractions and other reasons why the questionnaires may not have been distributed. The response rate varied between forces from 20 per cent to 58 per cent.

Appendix 4 : 'Bounty' payments to Special Constables

The idea of making some payment to Special Constables has been explored by several working parties convened since the 1960s on the grounds that payments might improve recruitment and retention. For example, a Scrutiny Report on the Special Constabulary was conducted in the Metropolitan Police Service (MPS) in 1988. It recommended an annual award to Specials who worked a minimum of 250 hours during the previous 12 months, with an enhanced payment for those who performed 350 or more hours of service. The advantages cited in support of the recommendation related not just to recruitment and retention but also the incentive to work more hours – especially for those Specials who were close to the thresholds for payment.

The Government decided that the option should be explored, and legislative provision for 'bounty' payments came into force in August 1992. A pilot scheme was set up to run in three forces, the MPS, Dorset and the City of London. Prior to the pilot scheme, Specials in these forces were surveyed to glean their opinion on the idea of payment for their work. Over 80 per cent expressed some support for the bounty; 40 per cent were 'quite a lot' or 'extremely' in favour. Those who were lukewarm or opposed to the bounty cited either concerns about losing their voluntary status, or said the size of the bounty was too low to be significant. Over 80 per cent also thought there would be some benefit to the force in terms of retention, increased commitment, morale and higher standards. Concerns were expressed by 60 per cent of respondents, notably that it might attract the wrong type of recruit or arouse antagonism on the part of regulars.

The Dorset experiment

For a number of practical reasons, Dorset was the only force to put the pilot scheme in place, and did so for a two-year trial period. The aims of the scheme were to:

– increase both the number and calibre of Specials recruited;

– encourage Specials to increase their time commitment to patrol duty and training, thus improving the service to the public; and

– reduce the number of Specials leaving the service.

The basic terms of the scheme were that Specials who worked 250 hours over a 12-month period (or 125 hours over 6 months) and satisfied other eligibility criteria qualified for a bounty of £400 (£200 for 6 months). Between October 1991 and September 1993 a total of £93,600 was paid to around 120 Specials, almost half of the force's establishment of Specials.

Dorset found the scheme difficult to administer for two principal reasons. Firstly, the force did not have in place a computerised system for recording the number of hours worked by each Special Constable; calculations had to be done manually and proved time-consuming. Secondly, staff were not equipped to answer queries relating to the payments, such as the effect on an individual's tax position. (Although there was pressure from some quarters to make the payments tax-free, this status was not granted). Some Specials may have been put off applying for the bounty because they were unsure whether they would actually benefit financially.

Dorset terminated its bounty scheme in 1993 following a thorough evaluation, which included a survey of some Specials. This found that around three-quarters of Specials agreed with the bounty payment, although the great majority felt it did not change their role in any way. There had been a significant increase in the hours worked by Specials, and the bounty was thought to be an effective means of expressing local communities' thanks for the service given by Specials. However, other key aims were not realised; there was, for example, little impact on recruitment or retention. The conclusion reached by the force management, and the Specials themselves, was that purchasing uniforms and equipment for the Special Constabulary would be a better use of resources than bounty payments of this sort.

References

Audit Commission, *Fine Lines: Improving the Traffic Warden Service*, HMSO, 1992

Audit Commission, *Helping with Enquiries: Tackling Crime Effectively*, HMSO, 1993

Audit Commission, *Cheques and Balances: A Management Handbook on Police Planning and Financial Delegation*, HMSO, 1994

David Bayley, *Police for the Future*, OUP, 1994

Lara Diez, *The Use of Call Grading*, Police Research Paper 13, Home Office, 1995

Electoral Reform Ballot Services, *Survey of Public Attitudes to Policing*, Police Federation, 1995

Professor Michael Hough, *Anxiety About Crime: Findings from the 1994 British Crime Survey*, Home Office Research Study No. 147, 1995

Rebecca Morley and Audrey Mullender, *Preventing Domestic Violence to Women*, Police Research Group Paper No. 48, Home Office, 1994

Lawrence Sherman et al, 'Hot Spots and Predatory Crime: Routine Activities and the Criminology of Place', *Criminology*, Vol. 27, 1989

Standing Conference on Crime Prevention, *Safer Communities: The Local Delivery of Crime Prevention through the Partnership Approach*, Home Office, 1991 (the Morgan Report)

Index References are to paragraph numbers

Abstractions	37, 87-9
Accessibility	86
Accountability	12, 41
Accreditation	111
Activity sampling	101
Agency co-operation	76
Anti-social behaviour	17-20
Auxiliary patrol officers	96
Beat managers	109, Case Study 3
Beat work	54
status of	59-61, 108-9
Bottom-up planning	44
Briefing and debriefing	107
shortcomings in style and content	55-8
Burglar alarms	28, 78
Burglary	17
Call grading.	*See* Graded response
Career development	109
CCTV	90, 94-5
impact of	94
evaluation of	95
safeguards against abuse	95
CID officers	55, 61
Citizen's Charter	77
Civilian staff	15, 84
Commitment	11, 113
Community safety	40, 69, 72, 74-8, 90
agency inputs	75-8
priorities for improving	76
Competence	18
Constable	
office of	1-3
Consumer panel	72

Control rooms	18, 19, 23, 25, 30, 31, 77, 85, 99
managing demand	80-4
monitoring	32-4, 82-3
performance evaluation	34
supervision	32-4
training needs	84
workload	33
Court attendance	37
Courtesy	18
Crime desks	31, 85-6
Crime investigation	50, 73
Crime Management Unit	85
Crime strategy	14
Crime victims, surveys of	18
Criminal behaviour	17
Debriefing. *See* Briefing and debriefing	
Demand gap	22
Demand management	87
Deployment criteria	30
Deployment decisions	25
Disorderly behaviour	51, 100
Dissatisfaction with response by patrol officers	19
Domestic violence	17, 52
Emergency calls	27, 32, 80, 83
grading	26-8
Emergency calls	
see also 999 calls	
Esprit de corps	55
False alarms	28, 78
Fast-response units	14, 28, 54
`Feel-good' factor	15, 16

Fieldwork forces	32, 44, Appendix 1
Fire-brigade policing	22-5
Foot patrol	2
dissatisfaction with current levels	9
image of	9
levels of	68
probationers in	65
public expectations	9-10
public preference for more	15-17
vs. patrol cars	16-17
Forward planning of abstractions	37
Fraud	17
Geographic policing	104-6
Graded response	24-34, 68, 80-6
applying it	24-34
criteria	81, 83
making it work	80-6
monitoring	82-3
variation between forces	27
Help desks	85-6
Home Office	69-74
Hot spots, analysis of	50
Immediate response	26, 28
Incident workload	21, 22, 33
increasing	35
Informal resolution	47
Information system	51
Inspectors	110
Intelligence gathering	54, 57
Intelligence officers	55
Intruder alarms	28, 78
Local authorities	76-7, 90

Local identification and ownership 53-4, 104

Local Intelligence Officers 57

Local Policing Plans 12, 58, 74

Mobile patrol 16

    see also Fast-response units

Monitoring 12, 32-4

    achievement 101-2

    graded response 82-3

    patrol outcomes 46, 47

National conditions of service 36

New York Police Department 50

999 calls 26, 70, 81

    see also Emergency calls

Non-crime calls 31

Non-incident time 43, 58, 64

Non-urgent incidents 29-31

Nuisance incidents 18-20, 51

Paperwork 15, 30, 63, 111

Partnership arrangements 40, 69, 72, 77, 109

Patrol cars 3, 6, 54

    double-crewing 35

    vs. foot patrol 16-17

    see also Mobile patrol

Patrol officers 60, 61

    briefing and debriefing 55-8, 107

    skill requirements 62-3

Patrol outcomes, difficulty of measuring 46-7

Patrol resources, unrealistic expectations 13-14

Patrol strength 5-6, 37

Patrol work

    additional contributions 90-3

    attitudes towards 61

briefing and debriefing 55-8, 107

    good practice 79-86

    key role 113

    levels of 13, 17

    limitations of 75

    local identification and ownership 53-4, 104

    nature of 8

    objectives 44-7

    organisation 4-6

    proactive 7, 22-4, 42, 44, 68, 79, 106, 108

    purpose of 9-11

    reactive 7, 22, 23, 42, 79

    setting objectives 98-100

    short-term focus 48-54

    status of 108-13

    supervision 62-4, 108-13

    targeting 97-107

    traditional basis of duty assignment 54

    transformation 3

    see also Foot patrol; Mobile patrol; Patrol cars

Performance indicators 58, 101-2

Personal radios 3

Planning processes 44

Police Act 1964 28

Police and Criminal Evidence Act 1984 20

Police authorities 69-74, 90

Police deployment 5

Police effectiveness 11

Police managers 17, 54, 102, 108

    concerns of 40

Police presence 9

Police priorities 4, 31

Police resources 4, 69

    matching to demand 24, 35-42

Police strength since 1900 1

Police visibility 15, 30, 45, 75, 76, 100

Priority search technique 72

Private sector 41

Private security guards 41, 90

Probationers 109

    assignment to training units 67

    tutoring 65-8, 112

Problem-solving 47

    ad hoc 49, 103

    approach 50, 53, 97, 103

    information technology 50-2, 103

Professionalism 11, 113

Public expectations 9-10, 12-14, 78, 79

Quality of service 31-3

Racial attacks Box C

Reassurance 12, 14, 22, 41, 44, 45, 69, 94, 100

Repeat victims or locations 51

Resource Desk 86

Response times 14

Scenario training 84

Sector policing 104

Security guards 41, 90

Self-assessment manual 81

Sergeants

    contact with constables 64

    roles of 63, 110, 111

Sheehy Inquiry 108

Shift arrangements 35, 36, 53, 56, 60, 87, 88

improved	87-9
traditional	53
Sickness absence	37, 89
Special Constables	24, 38-9, 90-2
as proportion of regular officer numbers	38
contribution of	92
duty commitment	39
retainer payment	92
skills profile	91
turnover	39
Specialised roles	5, 14
Specialist officers	6, 61
Supplementary provision	38-42
Surveys of victims and users	71
Team-based approach	99
Team ownership	104
Telecommunications	18, 73
Telephone demand	86
Telephone system	
effective handling of demand	86
operator pressure	33
role of	73
Traffic offences	58
Traffic wardens	90, 93
Training programme	66
Tutoring, probationers	65-8, 112
Vandalism	17
Working hours, changes to	36